THE
CARE AND KEEPING
OF
ANTIQUES

THE
CARE AND KEEPING
OF
ANTIQUES

by Epsie Kinard

Foreword by Marvin D. Schwartz

Greenwich House
New York

This 1982 edition is published by Greenwich House,
a division of Arlington House, Inc., distributed by
Crown Publishers, Inc. by arrangement with
Hawthorn Properties, a Division of E. P. Dutton, Inc.

Manufactured in the United States of America

Library of Congress Cataloging in Publication Data

Kinard, Epsie.
The care and keeping of antiques.

Reprint. Originally published: New York : Hawthorn
Books, [1972, c1971]
Bibliography: p.
Includes index.
1. Antiques—Conservation and restoration.   I. Title.
[NK1127.5.K5 1982]   745.1′028′8   82-9316
                                                  AACR2

ISBN: 0-517-385619

h g f e d c b a

TO RION, WITH LOVE

Contents

Foreword

IT IS GREAT TO SEE that here at last is a book on the care and maintenance of antiques which is presented in a format to guide the casual as well as the serious collector. The professional, whether a dealer or a museum curator, is able to consult the best conservators when he has a problem involving repairing, restoring, or cleaning, but the man with a small collection is left to decide for himself how to handle the inevitable problems that come up. This is a book with answers to many of the most difficult questions and, best of all, with warnings of when one should wait for professional assistance.

Taking care of objects one treasures is becoming increasingly important as they get harder and harder to replace. There was a time not too long ago when the charming mid-Victorian chair, the attractive little anonymous landscape, and a multitude of other accessories that fall into the category of the fine or decorative arts could be considered expendable. Often they did not cost much. When they got tattered or dirty, they could be discarded because substitutes were easy to find. Now, just as we are being made conscious of the fact that our natural environment is being destroyed by carelessness and wastefulness, the movement for preservation is being extended to include man-made objects. Our heritage in pictures, chests, and tankards is as important to many people as are the fabulous vistas our poets have described.

This book offers solutions to the problems of caring for objects people acquire for aesthetic delight or simply out of nostalgia. Aimed at the collector of trifles as well as treasures, it tells how to preserve pictures, furniture, silver, glass, and a myriad of other things that might or might not make it to a museum some day. Time-honored old methods and the latest techniques have been investigated by Epsie Kinard. She includes the best of both worlds. Some methods have never been questioned. On the other hand, many conservators bristle when anyone talks about "feeding" furniture. There are wonderful new ways to clean chandeliers, for example, using sprays that did not exist a few years ago, and sources for such new-fangled gadgets are listed in this book.

Whether the problem is big or small, the reader will be able to find a discussion that can assist him in developing an idea of how to proceed. Where elbow grease and a tricky combination of ingredients are all that is needed, he will find adequate directions. When the job requires unusual skill, he will be warned that a professional must be called upon. A book on preservation which tells one when to stop and when to go ahead will be of invaluable help, and *The Care and Keeping of Antiques* is a book that any collector can use.

Marvin D. Schwartz

Acknowledgments

THE AUTHOR ACKNOWLEDGES with gratitude the assistance of the following experts in the preparation of this book: Mrs. Carolyn Horton, hand bookbinder and specialist in the conservation of library collections, whose excellent book, *Cleaning and Preserving Bindings and Related Materials*, was the inspiration and source of Chapter 2; Mrs. Rita Ford, dealer in, collector of, and authority on antique music boxes, who shared her technical knowledge of the workings of their mechanisms; Miss Dorothy Chamberlain, who gave invaluable editorial assistance.

For their cooperation and willingness to share their knowledge and experience, I wish to express my deep appreciation to the following: Mrs. Susanne Sack, conservator, William Hanft, conservator of the Department of Prints, and Leon Rosenblatt, conservator of the Department of Primitive Arts, all of the Brooklyn Museum; Miss Alvena Seckar, art restorer, Pompton Lakes, New Jersey; Jonathan Fairbanks, associate curator of The Henry Francis duPont Winterthur Museum; Col. James W. Rice (U.S.A. Retired), consultant for textile conservation, Textile Museum; Dr. Martin Prager, supervisor of technical services, Copper Development Association, Inc.; Mme. Katy Maty, restorer of antique textiles; Michael Pell, Pell Studio, restorer of art and artifacts; Mrs. Beverly Reitz, interior designer; Samuel Pollock, glassmaker and glass-paperweight specialist; Erwin H. Ziegler, of Cliff Silver Company, restorer of antique silver, copper, and brass; Fritz von Waldenburg, ceramic restorer; George. Wells, master rug designer; and Al Thorp, gifted in furniture restorations.

I'm also indebted to the following organizations for their helpful cooperation: Sally Dickson Associates, National Pest Control Association, Louise Hand Laundry, Vermont Marble Company, Sterling Silversmiths Guild of America, Walter's Wicker Wonderland, and Veterans' Caning Shop.

E. K.

Introduction

AS ANCIENT AS YOUR ANTIQUE MAY BE, to you it is vibrantly alive. Therefore it needs the care that all living things demand. Emotionally, you respond to its unique beauty and to the deep significance of its place in history. Physically, though many generations of its owners have passed on, the antique is a link with the past. It should never be considered merely an inert and meaningless object.

To remain sound and to look its most handsome it needs faithful and loving attention. With appropriate and persistent care, your pampered antique will have a long life and will add the aura of its physical fitness to its beauty; with lack of attention, it may break down and deteriorate. How you can give antiques—from ivory miniatures to stone cupids the garden—the care they should have is the subject of this book. The information presented has been gathered from hundreds of authoritative sources.

The enemies of antiques are many. Time itself has inescapable effects, and an unfriendly atmosphere can disintegrate priceless leather bindings, corrode ancestral silver, spread a greasy film over oil paintings. Add to these adverse factors such problems as insect infestation, the excessive steam heat that warps and cracks antiques, and the "diseases" that sometimes affect bronze, brass, copper, and glass.

While tracking down the solutions to hundreds of problems and watching gifted craftsmen perform their minor miracles, I heard many experts say, "The less an amateur meddles with an antique, the better off it is." Other experts, however, passionately insisted—and showed examples to prove it—that a stitch in time can keep a century-old hooked rug from falling to pieces, that watchfulness and care can keep the fat folds of an American Aubusson from becoming the razor-sharp creases that cut the threads. In this day of scarcity of craftsmen it is more important than ever for the owner himself to deal with the simpler and recurring problems of antiques care. The most important rule he will be up against is that every effective cleaning process carries a risk. What removes dirt may also remove an unpredictable old finish. It's therefore axiomatic that you must go very easy and know when to stop.

Although antiques weren't made to cope with the conditions they face today, luckily they can profit from modern care techniques. Efficient new products have replaced old-fogy standbys that hadn't changed since Colonial times. The merits of cure-alls, such as linseed oil, have been scrutinized by newly critical eyes. For the first time it has been reported that a lovely patina will not continue to develop if you keep a patinated metal, stone, or wood antique in a cocoon of wax or lacquer.

Since no two problems are exactly alike, recommendations in this book must of necessity be of a general character. What may succeed for one type of antique may not for another. So remember that any formula given here must be modified to fit a particular piece and adapted to its own special needs.

THE
CARE AND KEEPING
OF
ANTIQUES

CHAPTER 1

Art in the Home

"DOTING OWNERS are often the worst troublemakers for their own works of art," says a restorer who undoes mistakes amateurs make. He claims they almost ruin paintings and prints in trying to clean them with such homespun remedies as sliced raw onions or fresh bread-crumbs. These novices hope to rescue a dazzling beauty's violet eyes and Renoir-like flesh tones from the muddy glaze of old varnish. With pressing and ironing, they struggle to uncurl old prints, or they attempt to bleach fox marks—frecklelike brown spots on century-old watercolors—at the risk of severe damage. If owners will follow good housekeeping practices, there is enough work to keep them busy without taking on any of the touchy tasks that should be left to experienced restorers.

OIL PAINTINGS

CLIMATE CONTROL

As important to paintings in the home as to flowers in a greenhouse is a stable climate—a year-round, unfluctuating relative humidity of around 50 per cent and a room temperature of between 70 and 72 degrees. When the humidity dips below 50 per cent, you can use a humidifier to restore moisture. You can measure the humidity of a room with a hygrometer—a museum's "watchdog"—and for control use a humidifier or a dehumidifier.

Although it is considered chic to turn a hot, vaporous bathroom or kitchen into a gallery, don't hang paintings in this overmoist atmosphere. Viewing your favorite Copley painting while you soak in a tub of perfumed foam or enjoying a cool green Catlin wilderness while you do kitchen chores will exact a heavy penalty from your art. Moisture invites fungus—a mold growth of cottony patches that feast on glue, sizing, and paint.

Lighting

Keep your works of art away from strong light as well. Direct sunlight, bright daylight, and fluorescent light have a deteriorating effect on oil paintings and will fade watercolors and injure the structure of the paper of prints. Either hang pictures where there's little or no exposure to strong light or keep window shades or curtains drawn.

If you wish to focus a light on a painting, throw a spotlight on it from across the room. This device is better for the painting and for viewing it than a reflector light mounted over the picture. A boxed reflector bulb may concentrate heat on the picture, and a light cord that tangles in a wad behind the picture may make the canvas bulge and the paint crack.

How to Hang a Picture

Hanging is a dramatic display technique, but choose your wall carefully, keeping the welfare of the picture in mind. Don't put a painting over the fireplace to be blasted by heat and fumes or over a hot radiator to suffer extremes of temperature. Instead of hanging a picture flat against the wall, a better way is inclining it from the top a few degrees. While you're at it, attach thin round slices cut from a cork to the lower corners of the frame to keep it away from the wall. This allows better circulation, and dirt will bypass the picture instead of settling on it. Most experts like to hang paintings at the eye level of the viewer when he is standing. They claim this makes pictures easier to see.

Checking up routinely on all the props used for hanging a painting—cords, wires, screws, hooks—will prevent its falling and receiving a hard bang. A severe blow can damage both canvas and frame.

CLEANING

The only cleaning an oil painting needs is a dusting occasionally with a soft brush three or four inches wide made of squirrel- and ox-hair bristles. Dust the frame (not the painting) with the round dusting brush of your vacuum. Never use a dust rag on a painting. Raveling threads can rip off lifted particles of paint.

WATERCOLORS

FRAMING

A watercolor is a brush painting on paper. Commonly but mistakenly it is glued to cardboard to give it solid support. During Colonial days the support might have been anything from strawboard to cedar shingles. If you have a watercolor worth preserving and it has been framed with a glued-on backing of cedar shingles or inferior cardboard, have it unframed, cleaned, properly mounted, and then reframed. In

How to clean an oil painting

expert hands it can be rescued from glue and cardboard damage and saved from ruin.

All too often glue comes up on the paper, seeps through to the watercolor, and takes off the paint. This can be avoided by backing a watercolor with museum cardboard of pure all-rag content. Unlike inferior grades of wood-pulp cardboard, it is free of chemical impurities. Your watercolor posed against it is safe, especially if damaging glue has been replaced by stain-proof gummed-tape hinges that adhere with cellulose paste. Used in attaching wallpaper, this paste is antifungus and has a pH of six (which is a chemistry symbol indicating slight acidity). So the backing board will hang free from the painting, have your framer place tape hinges at the top or at one side of the watercolor.

When you are having a watercolor reframed, consider having the glass replaced with ultraviolet filtration 3 acrylic plastic, which is a staple for filtering ultraviolet rays. No work of art should come in contact with the glass. Especially if you live in a coastal area, where dampness encourages

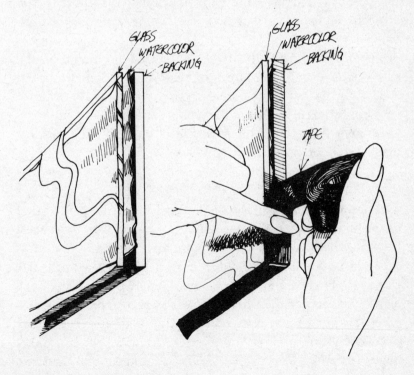

How to seal a watercolor

mildew and fox marks, be sure paintings do not touch the glass. In having a watercolor framed, see that painting, glass, and backing are sealed together with the adhesive to make one antidust unit. Unless such a barrier is erected, dust will work its way through to the watercolor paper.

LIGHTING

Watercolors are highly susceptible to fading. A concentration of strong light can turn a landscape's blue lake, blue sky, and field of yellow primroses into a bleached-out vista of ghostly white. Hang paintings away from direct sunlight and don't exceed fifteen footcandles of electric lighting at the point of hanging (the equivalent of two forty-watt fluorescent bulbs in a ten-foot ceiling). For short periods diffused or indirect light is best. This lighting for watercolors does not apply to occupants of the room, who may need the extra light of a shaded lamp for reading. For longer periods you might take your cue from a gallery expert. He removes framed watercolors from the walls in the spring and lays them away in a dark storeroom until winter's pale sunshine makes it safe to hang them again.

STORING UNFRAMED WATERCOLORS

Store unframed watercolors and prints flat in insect-proof drawers (ask your museum's paper conservator to suggest the insecticide to use) or in standard museum-type print cases large enough to hold them without crowding. The cases, which come in various sizes, are lined with all-rag acid-free paper. They help foil voracious paper-eating insects and are a safeguard against sulphur dioxide, soot, and dust. (See "Sources for Materials for the Care of Antiques," pages 149–150.) Interleaves of clear acetate of .003 thickness placed between watercolors or prints protect them from dirt and prevent friction. (See "Sources for Materials for the Care of Antiques," page 150.)

Controlling Climate

Guard watercolors against extremes of temperature and humidity. Like oil paintings, keep them away from fireplaces and radiators. To tackle dampness at its source give rooms in which watercolors hang or are stored frequent airings and plug in a dehumidifier that warms, dries, and circulates air.

PASTELS

Pastel, or dry-pigment, painting has the freshest charm and the most engaging fragility of any paper artifact, yet its delicacy makes it the most susceptible to destruction. Even brushing against a pastel as you pass by can take off a bit of evanescent color. Slamming the door of a room where a pastel hangs can shake off loose pigment in powdery heaps. As vulnerable to damage as a pastel is, however, it will respond to care very similar to that described for watercolors.

Cleaning and Framing

Besides framing, a pastel needs separating strips of cushioning material to keep it away from the glass. Sometimes a picture that touches the glass is transferred to it. A pastel cannot be cleaned, but the paper or parchment or rough white silk that supports it can be by a reputable paper-restorer. (Ask your museum curator to recommend one.) He will take the pastel out of the frame, correct any errors, clean the supports, or perhaps replace its old mounting with a better one. He also will seal together glass, pastel, and mounting as a barrier against dust.

Inhibiting Mold Growth

The restorer can be alerted in advance to include a mold-growth inhibitor. Ask him to back the new mounting with a sheet of camphor-treated blotting paper. To prepare it he will need to confine a sheet of blotting paper with a sprinkling of camphor crystals in an airtight package for a few days or a week. At the end of that time the blotter will be taken out and the pastel will have as a backing a uniformly permeated mold-inhibitor that has a life span of at least six months. The blotter will not need renewing if kept out of a high-humidity atmosphere. If it must be renewed, the entire sealed unit need not be disturbed. Only reopen the back of the unit, place the camphor-treated blotter in back of the mat, and reseal with pressure-sensitive tape.

Fixative: Pro and Con

If your pastel has never had a fixative applied to it, you might ask your restorer about the advisability of using one. A fixative is a special kind of invisible mat-finish spray for protecting the surface of a work of art. Some art experts take a strong stand against fixatives. Others laud the advent of new liquids in spray cans, which, if expertly applied, do not affect a picture's appearance and may stay the day when the lovely pastel color threatens to stray from the paper.

PRINTS

There are two safe places to keep prints: hanging on the wall in a proper mounting and frame or stored in a collector's cabinet or in portfolios, in contact only with materials that help halt deterioration.

FRAMING

If you're having valuable old prints framed or reframed, be sure you and your framer and mat-maker see eye to eye on the following points:

Frame a print with specially made protective ultraviolet filtration 3 acrylic plastic, slightly tinted amber, effectively used to filter ultraviolet rays. All kinds of light are enemies of prints.

Paper has few defenses against dust. Use them all. The finer dust is, the more it can penetrate and cut paper abrasively.

Both mat and backing board should be cut from all-rag acid-free cardboard, which has no chemical impurities. Any other kind of cardboard is liable to stain or bleed through onto the print.

Never let a print be bonded to a backing board as though it were a Polaroid photograph. Instead, for free hanging, have the print attached at the top or at one side to the backing with hinges of stain-proof gummed tape that adheres with cellulose paste. Combine print, mat, and backing board into one airtight, dustproof unit. Seal with the stain-proof cellulose adhesive. Such a nonstaining paste is as important as an all-rag backing board.

See that margins of prints get full play when matted, allowing ample space at the bottom for any legend, date, signature, or other visible mark of identification. Don't permit a framer to cut or trim a print in order to accommodate it to a smaller frame.

Keep a safe (even though infinitesimal) distance between print and glass. When there are temperature changes, moisture collects, and the print might otherwise stick to the glass when it dries. To keep the two apart use a deep mat or have a separating strip of rag board mounted at each side of the print.

Washing soiled glass would seem to be foolproof, but it can have disastrous effects if water penetrates to the print. To avert seepage place the print on a towel-covered cushion. Dip a washcloth in warm, soapy water, wring almost dry, and wipe the glass clean. Rinse with clean water and another nearly dry cloth.

Besides a framer, you may need an expert paper-restorer to clean, bleach, mend tears, repair holes, remove varnish, uncrease deep, dirty folds, or take the curl out of a rolled print. To find a reputable expert ask the curator of your museum to recommend one.

Light Protectors

A color print exposed to a couple of days of strong sunlight will show marked fading. A conservator is well aware of this fact. So take a leaf out of his notebook and keep your prints away from direct light and also from less-dangerous incandescent light. If you have a "gallery" of prints, rotate your collection, changing exhibits three or four times a year, or give your hanging prints a rest every six months.

The best lighting for wall-hung prints is thirty-five footcandles for overall room light, fifty or sixty footcandles for floodlighting. Although floodlights would seem to be hotter than room lights, their distance from the ceiling considerably reduces their heat and light. (One 150-watt floodlight bulb at a distance of eight feet equals approximately thirty-five to forty-five footcandles.) A room occupant can increase light with a well-shaded lamp, if need be, without increasing light on prints.

Custom-made Climate

Don't hang prints near radiators or air-conditioning vents. Although human comfort dictates room climate, the ideal relative humidity for prints (and watercolors and oil

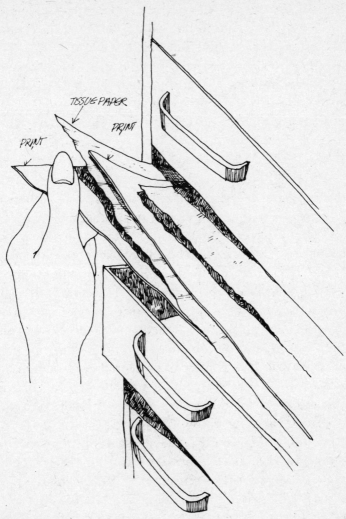

TISSUE PAPER

PRINT

PRINT

Storing prints

paintings) is between 40 and 50 per cent, and the right temperature is 68 to 72 degrees, an environment in which fungi, one of paper's worst ravagers, won't thrive. If the temperature goes higher, molds may flourish on the paper.

If the humidity goes lower, dryness and brittleness threaten. If the room is overmoist, the paper of nineteenth-century and older prints is in danger of foxing.

Dampness collects between pictures and the wall; this is also a happy hunting ground for mildew. This can often be avoided by creating better ventilation around the picture. Attaching a cork wedge to each corner of the frame will sometimes do the trick.

Safe Storage

Your collection can be in safe storage and at the same time viewable to admirers in a print cabinet or in map-type chests. Here you can stack prints, interleaving them with tissue paper or see-through sheets of clear acetate of .003 thickness. If the prints invite handling, give them the protection of rag-board folders or a rag-board support with a cover of the transparent acetate for see-through viewing and for keeping two prints from damaging each other. To make cabinet drawers more protective, line them with rag paper, as is done with the print cases favored by museums and collectors. Such cases resemble attaché cases, hold fifty prints, and are available in sizes ranging from $14\frac{1}{2}$ by $19\frac{1}{4}$ by $2\frac{1}{2}$ inches to 22 by 28 by $2\frac{1}{2}$ inches.

Prints for which you do not have a cabinet or case may be stored in cardboard tubes no less than three inches in diameter. Protect prints from acidic cardboard by rag paper, the face of the print by tissue paper. The safest area of the house in which to store prints is on the top shelf of a closet, where you can keep camphor crystals, a mild fungicide, which evaporate into heavier-than-air gas. If crystals are placed in an open dish in the upper part of a cabinet, the gas will mix with the air below.

CHAPTER 2

Leather Bookbindings

THE GOLD-TOOLED red morocco bindings of the Washington Irving novels handed down by your great-grandfather and the ruddy brown calfskin that binds your precious history of the Civil War are at the mercy of two implacable, unseen foes. The first—impurities, such as sulphur dioxide, in the air—is more destructive. As inexorable, however, are brittleness and the eventual powdery decomposition caused by gradual loss of the leather's natural oils. As hostile as these forces are, they can be stopped by preventive treatment.

Bindings made of calfskin or goatskin can be made acid-resistant to contaminants in the air by "wetting" them with a buffer-salt solution. This consists of 7 per cent potassium lactate, the buffer salt, and 0.25 per cent paranitrophenol, a mold-inhibitor. This is the famous formula developed at the British Museum. From it, Leather Protector is commercially made up and sold in this country at library-supply sources. (See "Sources for Materials for the Care of Antiques," page 150.)

Oil lost from leather bindings is replaceable with a leather dressing. Unless your library is air-conditioned, your leather bookbindings should be washed and oiled every two years. In a two-part treatment explained in detail below, you first wet the bindings with the buffer-salt solution, then pat on as much of the oily dressing as the leather will absorb. This ounce of prevention will save your treasured volumes before damage sets in.

To prepare books for this treatment give them a thorough dusting. Use a dustcloth or the round dusting brush of your vacuum cleaner. To hand-dust hold the book with the head-cap down. (The headcap is the covering leather that has been shaped over the headbands at the head and foot of the backbone of a hand-covered book.) Slant the spine up toward you and stroke the tops of the pages away from you with the dustcloth. Follow the same procedure if you are using a vacuum-cleaner brush. This is to prevent dust from sifting down between the leaves.

Apply the buffer-salt (potassium lactate) solution *only* to leather bindings of calfskin and goatskin. Suede, alum-tawed pigskin, vellum, or parchment call for other rules of care. (See "Treating Books with Peculiarities," page 32.) Caution: If the leather is dry and powdery, test it first by applying some of the buffer-salt solution on an inconspicuous area of the binding. If the leather turns dark, omit the solution and use only oil.

WETTING LEATHER BINDINGS

For full-leather bindings pour a small amount of the potassium-lactate solution into a glass dish. Use a cloth pad to pat it on. Hold the book in your left hand to keep it clean and dry while your right hand does the wet, messy work. Make sure that such vulnerable areas as headcaps and tail-caps and turn-ins at the top and bottom of the hinge boards are well moistened with the solution. When the leather has absorbed its fill, set the books vertically with their covers ajar and let them stand for half a day or so to dry. Bindings that are only partly leather are treated the same way, but more caution is required to keep the solution from staining the books' cloth or paper sides. This treatment prepares the leather for the oily dressing.

OILING LEATHER BINDINGS

To replace lost natural oils many rare-book experts use a particularly fine leather dressing that revitalizes the leather and gives it fresh tone. It combines two ingredients—neat's-foot oil (a pale-yellow oil derived from the feet and shin-bones of cattle) and anhydrous (waterless) lanolin—in 60–40 proportions. Typical of the users of this specialized leather dressing is famed library conservator Carolyn Horton, whose aid to flood-stricken Florence, Italy, a few years ago helped save millions of priceless books. (Her conservation practices can be found in her book *Cleaning and Preserving Bindings and Related Materials*, listed in the Bibliography on page 147.)

Ingredients for this leather dressing can be obtained from chemical-supply houses. To prepare it simply heat the lanolin over hot water in a double boiler and mix in the neat's-foot oil until they are blended into a clear, creamy emulsion. When the emulsion is cool, apply it with a cloth pad, a flat paintbrush, or your fingers. The method experts find most efficient is to grasp the entire body of pages firmly with one hand and to apply the dressing with the other. Two sheets of absorbent paper, such as yellow typewriter second sheets or copy paper, held against the flyleaves will keep oil off the pages as you work. Oil may darken bindings, especially those of porous leather, but this deepening of color is not considered undesirable. On some bindings it enhances the age-old patina.

After oiling a book, lay it on its side on a sheet of absorbent paper. Place two sheets of absorbent paper between books stacked on top of the first one. Allow a couple of days for the books to dry. Then examine each for arid areas, give any lackluster books another application of oil, and leave them a day or two longer to dry before polishing. The most favored rag for buffing up a shine is an old terrycloth towel worn soft. Replace it with a clean piece now and then to keep oil off book pages.

TREATING BOOKS WITH PECULIARITIES

Bindings of suede and powdery calfskin and goatskin leather need special care. Spray these with Krylon, a crystal-clear acrylic coating (see "Sources for Materials for the Care of Antiques," page 150), which helps protect leather and prevents powdery leather from disintegrating while leaving no visible sign of its presence. Clean alum-tawed pigskin and vellum or parchment bindings with a red rubber pencil eraser. Wipe artificial-leather bindings with a damp cloth.

GENERAL CARE OF BOOKS

Books react strongly to a room's climate, and it can help or harm them. They respond best to a relative humidity between 50 and 65 per cent and to a temperature that remains a constant 60 to 70 degrees. Air-conditioning and automatic dehumidifiers in a library mean your books will receive maintenance both day *and night*.

A library needs good circulation of air behind books stacked on shelves. Keep books away from direct heat and light—sunlight, incandescent light, and fluorescent light. If books are to be displayed, keep them away from strong light.

If a binding or the pages of a book are attacked by mildew—a mold growth of furry white patches—wipe off the growth with a soft, clean rag. That's also your cue to take your books out of the room to wipe, brush, sun, and air them before returning them to their shelves. Dry out the room with an electric dehumidifier or fans to halt the spread of mildew. If small orangey-brown spots reveal foxing on pages, consult an expert.

Don't pull at the top of the spine to remove a book from a shelf. Push its closest neighbors on either side toward the back of the shelf, leaving the one you want free. Keep books that only partially fill shelves upended and supported by bookends to prevent the damage that sprawling can do to a spine. Don't have a valuable book rebound unless it is disintegrating and a new binding will save it.

CHAPTER 3

Brass, Bronze, and Copper

THE HOME AND GARDEN owe much of their radiance through the centuries to the rosy glow of brass, bronze, and copper. Though these three metals belong to the same family and have many similarities, there are enough differences to make a strong individual out of each one.

Old brass is found in many beautiful forms, from giant apple-butter kettles to candle-lit chandeliers upon which distinguished smiths of Colonial days were proud to put their marks. An alloy of copper and zinc, brass has been used extensively since very ancient times: The first trumpet, mentioned in the Book of Job of the Old Testament, was made of it. Bronze, an alloy of copper, tin, and sometimes lead, has for millennia enchanted collectors of the small figures, particularly those of animals, lovingly wrought from it by sculptors. Copper, an unalloyed element, may be found in the form of a warming pan as shapely as a banjo or a weathervane of the archangel Gabriel blowing his horn. It also adds glory to the kitchen, with rows of gleaming pots and pans. The exceptional treasure that all three antique metals bring to their owners today is a matchless patina, the beautiful blue-green offspring of time and air.

BRASS

Patina versus Polish, Wax, and Lacquer

Everyone wants a patina. It increases the value of an object, adds to its beauty, stamps it with a bloom of maturity and dignity which age-old things possess, and sometimes establishes evidence of antiquity. A patina takes from eight to twenty years to develop, and sometimes it never does. If it is destroyed, the process must begin anew, and patination may never satisfactorily develop.

One of the dangers in cleaning brass is that a patina can be grazed off with coarse powder and brutal rubbing or burnished away with a polishing tool. So clean patina only with a light hand and let corrosion in hollows and scroll-work remain. As one chemist realistically puts it: "What is patination but corrosion's lovely blue-green touches?"

The patina on your elegant brass table or candelabrum will not continue to develop if you keep it in a cocoon of wax or lacquer. These coatings fight off patination by creating a barrier between the metal and the atmosphere. Also, in removing wax or lacquer, you may strip off any earlier patina.

Of course, there is more reason for patina on old brass used for display than on utility pieces. The cleaner and brighter a kettle's gleam, the more inviting it looks on a table set for tea. You may have to decide whether the greater virtue is a weathered patina or a clean brightness achieved with polish and elbow grease.

Wash Before You Polish

You can spare yourself much tiresome rubbing on large shiny-surfaced pieces if you wash them in hot water and soapsuds with a little ammonia added before polishing. Then rub on polish with a soft cotton-flannel cloth, wash in hot suds, rinse, and dry thoroughly. Note: All residue from polish, except those that contain tarnish-preventatives, should be washed off metal pieces immediately after cleaning to prevent rapid retarnishing.

Cleaning Ornamental Objects

Small decorative pieces with much intricate detail— embossed tobacco boxes, heavily scrolled picture frames, engraved inkstands—should not be cleaned with cream or powder brass polishes, which tend to leave a residue in moldings and deeply recessed crevices. If there's a patina in these grooves, don't touch them; clean only the high-relief planes. Use salt moistened with a little hot vinegar to make a paste and apply it with a soft cloth. Wash off the salt-and-vinegar paste with warm, soapy water, then rinse, dry, and polish with a soft cloth.

Cleaning Blackened Fireplace Tools

Uncovering the sparkle of brass under layers of pitch-black resin can be as rewarding as finding the marble head of a Greek goddess while on an archaeological dig. To find out what kind of brass lurks beneath, experiment on the underside or on the base of an andiron. Use a heavy-duty brass polish and a pad of steel wool. Gleaming rays shining through from this initial scrubbing should give you clues as to the quality of brass, the kind of cleaner it will need, and what kind of job is ahead of you.

You may have to tackle the stripping job again and again with emery paper and heavy-duty brass polish, going over stubborn patches of burned-in resin until they vanish. This Herculean chore may be speeded up by using stainless-steel or copper wool. If the brass has a scratch-brushed finish, it can take abrasive treatment. Do not, however, use these wools on fireplace tools with a high polish. To protect the polished finish use a nonabrasive cream metal cleaner with a soft cloth. When the black coating is finally stripped, wash polish off the fireplace tools with hot soapsuds, rinse with clear hot water, and dry thoroughly.

CLEANING BRASS-INLAY ORNAMENTATION

You can clean buhlwork (brass insertions that decorate furniture) with a fine emery cloth and brass polish. Keep a good grip on the emery cloth so it can't tangle with the brass and rip it out.

HOLDING TARNISH AT BAY

For brass with no patina to guard, apply a clear, hard paste wax, such as the kind you use on your automobile. Film it on smoothly and uniformly.

CLEANING LACQUERED BRASS

Dust the piece, then wipe it clean with a damp cloth. When a coating of soil accumulates, wash it off with light, warm soapsuds, rinse, and dry. If the lacquer film cracks, it should be removed; air admitted through the cracks can cause tarnishing in patches.

Stripping Lacquer

Use a cloth or brush to apply a lacquer-thinner or -stripper. To rub off the lacquer switch to a coarser cloth, such as terrycloth. Then wash the brass with warm, sudsy water and dry.

Relacquering

Turn this job over to an expert. It is useful, however, to know which lacquer among the hundred or so products on

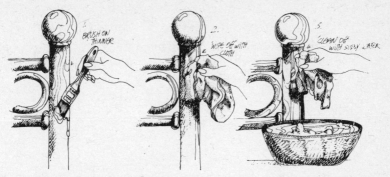

Stripping lacquer from brass

the market will work best for your brass. (Ask your paint-dealer's advice.) Lacquer for a sundial, for instance, should be of higher quality than that for the samovar brought home by an ancestral sea captain. Outdoors, lacquer is subject to the deteriorating effects of strong sunlight and extremes of weather.

Smashing the Myth of "Rebrassing"

So-called rebrassing of old locks, doorknobs, escutcheon keyhole shields, and similar ornaments that seem worn bare in spots is actually simply a matter of buffing and polishing to restore brassy brightness. If the brass is lacquered, the lacquer must be stripped. What appear to be worn-down areas may be only spots of heavily encrusted tarnish. Although drastic measures may be required, an expert can remove these spots with electric buffing tools.

Authentic Reproductions of Brass Hardware

If you need to find and have copied hardware of any period—handles, knobs, hinges, hasps, locks—consult your local museum. Its conservators may also guide you to brass founders whose specialty is replacement of missing parts. They may have both originals and reproductions from various periods in their collections: brass shoes for the legs of a Duncan Phyfe table, rosette handle knobs for a Sheraton desk, teardrop handles for William and Mary dining-room pieces, or whatever you need for restoring your prize antique.

BRONZE

PATINA

This pleasing aspect of metallic corrosion is not to be confused with oxidation. Although both are the result of chemical changes, one is desirable, one is not. Oxidation is the dulling film of tarnish that forms when oxygen combines with metal. Patina is the stable and highly desirable film or encrustation that forms naturally on the surface of metals (also wood, stone, marble, ivory) to give them unusual texture and coloring. A patina makes objects so blessed by nature more aesthetically appealing and more valuable. A patina may form a thin, hard film like an enamel covering on a Victorian snuffbox, or it may be heavily encrusted. It can stun you with the spectacular beauty of its coloring, as patinas range in hue from pale turquoise to the nearly silver-white of the ancient Chinese bronzes, three thousand years old yet still exciting the admiration of the world.

A strong patina with a good color can take more polishing and burnishing than a weak patina. An engaging design about to be lost under a cherished blue-green deposit can be brought up by light polishing, however, without any harm to the patina.

WAXING BRONZE AND COPPER

Don't use wax if you want the metal to patinate. Wax slows down a patina or, by excluding air, prevents one from forming.

"Bronze Disease"

On occasion owners of art bronzes encounter "bronze disease" or "collector's plague." Although what causes this is not well understood, the light-green splotches—sometimes crumbly and moist, sometimes powdery—that break out in a rash on a bronze, copper, or brass object can eventually destroy it. If these symptoms occur, ask your museum's advice about treatment.

Cleaning

For bronzes the unwelcome signs of oxidation can be removed with regular cleaning. The cleaning ritual is gentle: Dust once a week with a soft cloth and once a month with a soft-bristled brush to sweep dirt out of hollows and crevices.

Polish afterward with a clean cotton-flannel cloth or

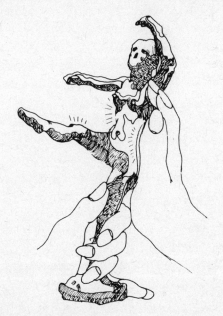

Polishing bronze with the palm

with the palm of your hand, as the Chinese do. Polishing a small bronze with the oil from your hand will work up a matchless gleam on the curves of a dancing girl or the contours of a child's head and cheeks. Any good but gentle commercial cleaner or polish—one usually cleans, the other brings up and preserves a shine—will remove spotty oxidation stains, but be careful that the ones you choose won't scratch the bronze.

OUTDOOR SCULPTURE

The bronze sculptures that brave the elements on a wall, in a garden, or as a grinning Bacchus holding up a birdbath need protection against exposure. Before severe weather sets in, wash the sculpture with a brush and soap and water, to which a little ammonia has been added to cut greasy film. Rinse, dry thoroughly, and polish with a soft, clean rag dipped in olive oil, lemon oil, or boiled linseed oil (you buy it boiled). Remove all surplus oil with a second clean cloth and a brisk rubbing.

Oiling outdoor sculpture two or three times a year develops a protective film against the elements and cleans away collected soot. The stains from snow and its aftermath of salty slush can be removed by more rubbing with an oily rag. The bronze statue of Alice in Wonderland in New York's Central Park owes its spit-and-polish gleam to routine maintenance stints with an oily rag, and so do Lorenzo Ghiberti's famous bronze doors of the Baptistery in Florence, Italy.

LACQUERED BRONZE

This needs only to be dusted and wiped occasionally with a damp cloth. If the lacquer film cracks or peels, strip it. (See instructions for stripping and relacquering under "Brass," pages 38–39.)

COPPER

If it's copper, it is made of a pure metal—sometimes included among the "noble" metals—with a five-thousand-year record of challenging the skills of artist and craftsman.

CLEANING

Copper is highly susceptible to scratches. If you are its caretaker, use one of the good, nonabrasive copper cleaners or use jeweler's rouge, a fine red powder that helps jewelers ply their delicate craft. Be careful to keep the powder out of the grooves of engraved pieces. If crevices are deep, you can shield them from powder or paste by packing them temporarily with dampened facial tissues.

Copper, like brass and bronze, takes an esteemed patina, and like silver it is tarnished by sulphur impurities in the air. If moisture is compounded with the air, oxidation is rapid, leaving a dark, dulling film on the object. If not halted, the film may change to a green deposit like that you see on domes and roofs of buildings. In any of these states except deep oxidation, routine cleaning will restore copper's brightness.

Stubborn stains will respond to a commercial copper polish or a paste made of equal parts of salt, flour, and hot vinegar. Rub it on the offending spots. After cleaning, wash the piece thoroughly, rinse well, and dry.

COOKING UTENSILS

The glory of a gourmet kitchen full of antique copper pots, pans, long-handled skimmers, and punchwork colanders swinging from butcher's hooks is sometimes dimmed by oxidation. To remove the green carbonate compound that collects on such utensils wash them in several changes of soapsuds. To a sinkful of hot-water soapsuds add a teaspoon of ammonia. Keep affected utensils scrupulously clean after the crusty particles have been removed.

Corrosion explains why the reaction of vegetable acids and copper imparts an unpleasant metallic taste and why copper cooking vessels must be lined with a thin coating of tin. When the lining splits or wears down, the utensil must be retinned.

LACQUERED COPPER

Once copper has been lacquered, there's no way to clean it except with soap and water. If it becomes a dull captive of a lacquer film, the only thing to do is to strip it. (See instructions for stripping and relacquering under "Brass," pages 38–39.)

CHAPTER 4

Crystal Chandeliers

UNTIL MODERN TECHNOLOGY came to the rescue of crystal chandeliers, cleaning one of these fairylike creations was a drippy mess, with a washpan planted on acres of newspapers spread out below. Out of a photographer's lab comes a dry and tidy way to clean a cascade of prisms. Chemistry goes a step further and fills spray cans with cleaners specially devised for crystal chandeliers. These cleaning methods and two others are described below.

AIR-BLASTING

A housewife can make as good use of compressed air as can a commercial photographer by directing a powerful stream of it at a dirty chandelier. That's the instant-cleaning way photographers blast dust off camera backs, film holders, and negatives. Ask at camera shops for Omit, the compressed-air spray photographers use for cleaning their cameras, or order it from Peerless Camera Shop. (See "Sources for Materials for the Care of Antiques," page 150.)

Air-blasting a chandelier

DRIP-DRY WASHING

Without rinsing, wiping, or polishing, you can "wash" a chandelier. Ask for crystal-chandelier cleaner. Before using, spread newspapers out on the floor below the chandelier in order to catch the drips. Spray the cleaner from the aerosol can onto the chandelier and let it dry. (See "Sources for Materials for the Care of Antiques," page 150.)

WINDOW-CLEANER WASHING

A liquid window-cleaning spray that instantly cleans glass can be used on a crystal chandelier. This staple spray is sold at supermarkets. Wipe each prism clean and dry with paper towels, as you do a windowpane. The moment a towel becomes soiled, replace it with a fresh one.

CLEANING DISMANTLED PARTS

The key to dismantling a chandelier so that parts can be washed, polished, and put back together is the small wire pin (or hook) that suspends a crystal or links it to another. When these pins are dissolved by rust, a crystal drops and may be broken or lost. Pins of malleable brass or silver wire are available at glass-repair shops, ranging in length from three-fourths of an inch to two inches. Some people prefer to make their own pins, using brass or silver wire bought by the yard and snipping it with scissors to desired lengths. Pins should be hooked up while the chandelier is dismantled.

Wash a disassembled chandelier as you would fine glass, using soap flakes dissolved in warm water to which a small amount of bluing is added for sparkle. Rinse in clear, hot water and dry and polish each piece with lintless paper towels, one in each hand.

Those missing parts that make otherwise dazzling chandeliers look like Belle Époque beauties in ragged dress can be replaced. Glass-repair shops, antique dealers, and auction houses often have prisms, teardrops, bobeches, chains, even candle arms (arms branching out from the central stem of a chandelier) that match yours.

When taking down and rehanging crystal parts, heed this

warning: Don't turn a chandelier to accommodate your fixed position on a ladder. Instead, move the ladder around the chandelier. By thoughtlessly turning a chandelier counterclockwise, you can unscrew it from the ceiling and risk its crashing to the floor.

For brass and iron chandeliers and candelabra see the section on brass in Chapter 3 and "Iron," Chapter 11. For product suppliers see "Sources for Materials for the Care of Antiques," page 150.

CHAPTER 5

Clocks

IF YOUR ANTIQUE CLOCK was made before Waltham, Massachusetts, began turning out three hundred clocks a day on an assembly line in around 1865, you have an irreplaceable treasure. Now, as in the days of Colonial craftsmen, a banjo, mantelpiece, looking-glass, lighthouse, or grandfather clock is valued as a piece of fine furniture as well as a good time-keeper. The owner of an antique clock must have strong defenses against dirt, wear, and any temptation to tamper with its works.

THE CLOCK

Familiarity with the clock's rhythms will help you take better care of it. Listen to it tick. An even tick-tock is a sign that all is well; an uneven beat is a warning that something has gone awry and needs to be checked. If you have a pendulum clock, a searching glance now and then to see that the pendulum stays level is good caretaking.

Have your clock checked once a year by a specialist in the repair of antique clocks. Although their ranks are thinning, there are still a few repairmen who served their apprenticeships by taking old clocks apart and putting them together again. Your expert will clean out dirt-congealed oil, which makes movements sluggish and causes bearings and pinions to clog. Such a checkup can postpone or even avoid an expensive overhauling.

THE CLOCK CASE

Dust the case once a week with cheesecloth moistened with a little polish. If the case is wooden, use a wood-enriching furniture cream polish; if silver, brass, or bronze, use metal polish to remove tarnish. Wipe the case free of polish with a damp cloth and dry thoroughly.

The oil used for lubricating the mechanism attracts dust, so keep an eye on the ports of entry. Any cracks should be filled with wood filler or covered with heavy paper glued on the inside. Fabric linings for ornamental openwork panels, originally intended to filter out dust, should be renewed when they give way.

To preserve the wood of an antique clock case wax it once a year, as you would other fine wooden furniture. If it has grown dry or brittle, apply oil on the raw wood of the clock-case interior. Use a mixture of one-half boiled linseed oil and one-half kerosene. Apply it with a paintbrush, taking care not to touch any of the clock's mechanisms. Woods such as soft pine and poplar will sop up this oil mixture like a sponge. Mahogany, walnut, and other hardwoods may not absorb much oil at first but will drink in more on a second or third application. In any event, oil brushed on the inside is not apt to penetrate the outside finish of your clock case.

If the outside finish is crazed (has a network of minute cracks), marked, or gouged, you may want an expert to give the case a French polish—to gloss it and make uneven surfaces uniform. Under no circumstances should this method of applying multiple layers of shellac until a hard, glasslike shine is achieved be attempted by an amateur. If you think, as many do, that the marks of age and wear on a venerable clock are more distinguished than a glossing with French polish, forgo the finish. Settling for a mellowed patina is usually a more discriminating choice.

Don't trust your amateur skill to wash the face of a hand-decorated clock. The face was often a favorite place for an artist to paint a miniature watercolor or to gild or silver the hour ring, the outer ring of the disk holding the numerals. To safeguard these quintessential grace notes of antique clocks let a dusting suffice. Wash only the other side of the painted glass panel or door.

If a reverse painting on a glass panel—the picture that is painted to be seen through the glass—is smashed, the broken glass can be replaced by a glazier, or an artist can duplicate

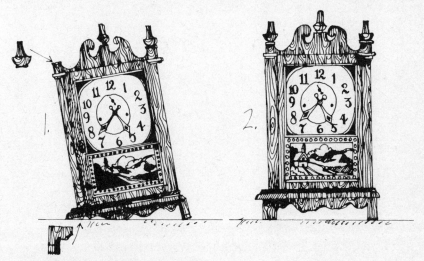

Restoring an antique clock

the painting on eighteenth-century European white glass—perhaps a pastoral landscape, picture-book church, or graceful shepherdess—and recapture the pristine glory of the original. Missing parts—knobs, door latches, feet, carved finials crowning a graceful arch—can be replaced by a skilled cabinetmaker or wood-carver. So can fragile wood ornaments that have been knocked off, as well as inlays of pearl, shell, or brass which have sprung loose from their beds of dried glue. You can have the dial resilvered or varnished, a pendulum's lost bob replaced, and new clockworks put into an old case, all by experts skilled in antique-clock repairs.

CHAPTER 6

Frames

THE FUNCTION OF THE FRAME that encloses the fantasy world of a painting or the magic reflecting pool of a mirror is as a target for the eye. Yet not until the seventeenth century, when sheets of glass became larger, did frames assume their rightful importance as objects of art in and of themselves—as architectural styles, as gesso-decorated molding, as the richest ornaments on a wall—not merely auxiliaries to works of art. Taking care of Renaissance-rich frames—of gold or silver leaf, tortoiseshell, ivory, mother-of-pearl, lacquer, and hand-carved woods—when there were no standardized rules posed both a challenge and a responsibility to owners of these antiques. Today we have learned how to take care of them.

GOLD LEAF

Classic gilding fixes a thin skin of pure gold—eighteen to twenty-three karats—on a ground of gesso (the Italian term for plaster of Paris) molded and glued to the frame's wood. (The word "gilding" is also applied to metallic leaf, metallic pastes, and gold-colored paint, but none should be mistaken for pure gold.) In spite of its veil-like thinness, gold leaf provides a sturdy coating, one that will never tarnish.

Unless a frame is heavily soiled, let dusting suffice. Use a clean, dry shaving brush. Its long, soft bristles seem tailored for the job of flushing out dirt settled in the frame's carving. A brush is preferable to a dustcloth, which can loop around scrollwork and yank off a section of it.

If a gilded frame needs more than routine dusting, test the back or some other inconspicuous area with a dry-cleaning fluid. Moisten an absorbent cotton swab with the fluid and gently roll it on or pat the gold leaf—don't rub or scrub. Leave the tested area alone for a day or two so you can judge the reaction. Continue only if it is completely favorable. This method was recommended by a museum, provided it was tested first.

If there are worn-away or mottled spots, either accept these ravages of time as inevitable or have the gilding renewed by an expert. He can apply fresh gold leaf to look like the old. Don't try to touch up these spots yourself. The results could wreck a valuable old frame.

SILVER LEAF

Basically the same method used for gilding is used for silvering with pure silver leaf. Through the years, however, silver leaf suffers what never happens to gold leaf: a total blackout from tarnish. The only recourse is to have the frame resilvered. Don't try to restore brightness with aluminum paint. Just as with gilded frames, silvered ones can be maintained by dusting with a clean, dry shaving brush.

TORTOISESHELL

If the frame has an easel back with a facing of tortoise-shell screwed to it, dismount it by unscrewing the shell. To clean and rejuvenate the shell submerge it in hot, pure olive oil and rub off soil and stains with a cotton-flannel polishing cloth. For persistent stains lift out the shell and rub damaged spots ever so lightly with putty paste (putty powder moistened with a little water). Then return it to the oil bath. Remove the shell from the oil and let it stand for twenty-four hours to absorb oil. At the end of that time, the shell will be dry enough for polishing with another cotton-flannel polishing cloth.

If tortoiseshell is firmly attached to a mirror backing, don't submerge it. Clean it with an oil-dipped cloth. Again, let it stand for twenty-four hours before polishing.

Flushing dirt from an ivory frame with a shaving brush

IVORY

Wipe ivory clean with a sponge dipped in warm water and wrung out almost dry. Take care not to get the frame even moist. Water causes ivory layers to separate. Rub dry with a cotton-flannel cloth.

Don't tamper with decorations except to flush dust out of deep carvings with a clean, dry shaving brush or other soft, long-bristled brush. Don't try to lighten a yellowish tinge; this comes naturally to ivory.

MOTHER-OF-PEARL

Gentle swabbing with absorbent cotton balls dipped in suds made of pure soap flakes and warm water and wrung out almost dry will lift much surface soil from mother-of-pearl inlays and all-over decorations. On stubborn stains use a damp cotton swab dipped in a little pumice powder. Rinse well with a clean wad of cotton moistened in clear, warm water and wrung out almost dry.

LACQUER

See instructions for the care of lacquer in Chapter 7, "Furniture."

CARVED WOOD

Clean wooden carvings with a soft, long-bristled brush. If the fine wood—ebony, mahogany, chestnut, teak, or whatever—has lost its luster because of too many layers of wax, strip off the wax, dirt and all, with turpentine swabbed on with cotton.

You may not need to do anything else. If you wish to finish with a new coat of wax to help keep the frame clean, protect it, and add luster, however, apply a natural paste wax with a clean cotton-flannel cloth and rub until the gleam comes up. Keep wax out of the carvings. Dust the frame once a week with another clean cotton-flannel cloth.

CHAPTER 7

Furniture

A PEEK INTO THE CLEANING PANTRY of an early-American home would explain how the lady of the house started her elegant custom-made furniture down the road to posterity. Except for a polishing rag torn from the tail of a worn-out nightshirt, all her pantry boasted was a tin can of beeswax, which she herself had made of honeycomb melted in boiling water, strained, cooled, and mixed with turpentine.

Compared with today's unlimited battery of push-button products, where a squirt of an acrylic spray is the equivalent of an hour of hand-rubbing, her arsenal had to make up in muscle power—an inexhaustible supply of elbow grease— what it lacked in quantity and variety. The early scarcity of cleaners and polishes contributed to the hand-rubbed beauty of old pieces. Hand-power, a hard fact of life in Colonial times, is today a tribute of love and patience paid to old furniture to help it preserve its beauty and live a long and useful life. The following instructions on care cover the various categories of antique furniture.

HIGH-STYLE

This furniture will be recognized by its refined cabinet-work and elegant hardwoods—mahogany, walnut, rosewood, fruitwood, cherry, maple, butternut, and others. The beauty of its finish depends on how much hand-rubbing you are willing to devote to making it shine with a high gloss or gleam in a low key.

Regular dusting with a soft, clean cloth and periodic waxing and polishing are all the care required. Surface flaws can be masked with pigmented liquid wax, available at hardware and paint stores in a range of tones to match furniture woods. Such wax carefully applied—follow manufacturer's directions—can fill in scratches and conceal rings or stains with color.

If there is no necessity for pigmented wax—or if you scorn the cover-up—this furniture can be waxed sparingly once every six months with a hard paste wax. Hand-rubbing with a soft cotton-flannel cloth will bring up a high gloss. Avoid waxing too lavishly, as this will cloud the finish or gum up the patina. Between wax applications hand-rubbing to remove soil and smudges will work wonders in keeping a finish lustrous.

Marquetry decorations—inlaid designs of contrasting exotic woods—can be kept from becoming bone-dry by lubricating and cleaning them now and then with a little olive oil. Apply with a cotton-tipped toothpick or match and rub with a soft, clean cloth, taking care not to smear adjoining wood. Remove any surplus oil with a dry cloth and then polish.

The surface of fine hardwoods has a tendency to lose color with age. Don't let this panic you into using such restoratives as colored waxes. Soft-focus tones are a mark of precious patina.

OIL-FINISHED

Country pine, poplar, and oak, if dry and unsealed, require oil plus rubbing for that coveted oil-rubbed finish. Besides lubricating dry wood, oil enriches the grain, which makes the furniture look warm and alive. It will change the appearance of these unsealed woods, generally by darkening them; however, they look handsomer when regularly oiled.

The oil dressing used by conservators at the Brooklyn Museum—one-third vinegar, one-third turpentine, one-third boiled linseed oil—to clean and rub up a gleam is applied with a dampened cloth. Never pour the dressing directly on the wood. After waiting for a couple of hours for the oil to be absorbed, any surplus should be wiped off with a clean, dry, soft rag.

The use of boiled linseed oil, as suggested here, came up for critical examination at a meeting of the Scientific Advisory Committee of The Henry Francis duPont Winterthur Museum in 1969. Because of the scrutiny focused on this old standby by leading conservation experts and their knowledgeable and sparing use of it—"You put on three parts and wipe off six," according to one critic—linseed oil should be used only with full knowledge of its potential dangers.

In two or three days, for example, the oil sets and hardens. Therefore, wipe it off the same day it is used. Also, being a polymerizing varnish, linseed oil dries slowly, grows hard and horny, and becomes yellow. In time, you cannot remove it with ordinary solvents. For these reasons, don't let linseed oil build up over a long period unless the permanent finish it creates is just what you prefer.

Unless oil-finished furniture receives hard or abrasive wear, dusting is all the regular care it needs. Glaring scratches, rings, and stains can be removed with the lightest going-over with fine steel wool, slightly moistened with furniture oil or boiled linseed oil. Wipe afterward with a clean cloth. The rule is: Never use wax on furniture that you oil.

PAINTED

Whether the hand-painted designs are artist-signed primavera panels on headboards, portraits of Shakespearean characters on cabinets, or birds, flowers, angels, and unicorns on Pennsylvania Dutch hope chests, the glory of such furniture is the decoration, sealed fast by protective coats of spirit varnish. These engaging motifs of the past are there to stay if you keep the protective lacquer from wearing away. Once it goes, the character, color, and charm of the painted decoration will go, too.

Give painted furniture a dusting when necessary, using only a clean, soft, grit-free cloth. A painted piece that has become unduly soiled can be washed, but only with great care. With this caution in mind, wash with a very mild soap and warm water and a soft, clean cloth, free of grit and other abrasives. Wring the cloth almost dry and wash a small section of the painted surface. Rinse with a second cloth dipped in clear water and dry thoroughly with another cloth. Then go on to the next small area. If the wood or the background gets wet, there is danger of the paint lifting off, so be careful in washing.

Wax your painted furniture lightly with a spray wax every three or four months; don't use linseed oil. It destroys the paint's natural appearance. True, linseed oil can heighten the patina—but at the expense of the wood's becoming darker. Never use linseed oil on gold leaf, either, for it would discolor it.

LACQUER

Lustrous lacquer—of which an eighteenth-century fancier said the smallest piece was worthy of a place in the grandest palace—owes its Oriental glitter to a natural varnish made from the sap of an Oriental sumac tree. To make furnishings of it many layers of lacquer, treated with jet-black or colored pigment, are applied to a base of paper or thin wood.

Forget about cleaning lacquer furniture with a damp cloth, which is the first thing people usually reach for when they see a smudge or fingerprints. When moistened, a wooden base may swell and reject the lacquered surface. If the foundation is paper, moisture may cause loss of the paper's sizing, which might make the lacquer peel.

For a light cleaning of surface soil and smudges, a museum curator claims success with a household spot-remover, wiped on with a soft, clean cloth and removed instantly. To lift a dulling film use a homemade paste of flour and olive oil, applied with a soft, clean cloth and rubbed on with a circular motion. After wiping off the paste, polish briskly with an old nylon stocking.

To restore luster to lacquer, a crystal-clear acrylic coating (Krylon) that leaves no visible sign of its presence can be sprayed on. A normal butyl-methacrylate varnish (Synvar) is perhaps better for a glossy finish, although it does scratch easily.

WICKER

Antiques made of willow's pliable twigs, among the most attractive imports from the Far East during the days of the

Wetting down wicker furniture

China trade, strongly resist the ravages of time in spite of
their fragile openwork structure. Wash only natural, unpainted wicker. To clean and bring up its color, mix a
tumbler each of peroxide and vinegar into a pail of water
and apply the solution with a sponge. Rinse with clear water
and let the furniture dry thoroughly before using it. Dust
painted wicker regularly with a damp rag and clean it with
a sponge and clear water a couple of times a year.

Wetting down wicker furniture—painted and unpainted—
once a year with a garden hose or under a shower will slake
the willow's thirst and keep it from drying out or splitting.

If you don't have a backyard and if using a shower is not feasible, do what affluent Chinese families did on the eve of a vacation. They covered their wicker with layers of wet newspapers, a ritual likely to preserve moisture until their return.

Before repainting, you can dampen wicker this way to clean it. Then let it dry thoroughly. Also before repainting, file off the "whiskers," the fuzzy fibers roughed up with wear. Rub with very fine (000) sandpaper, following the lines of the grain, or you can flame off the fuzz with fireplace matches or tapers of tightly twisted newspaper in very much the same way that your grandmother used to singe off a chicken's pinfeathers.

Repaint, using a spray paint with a plastic base. Repeat with another coat if you'd like a smoother finish or a deeper color. Every coat (you can hardly give a piece too many) enhances wicker furniture's good looks and helps preserve it.

BAMBOO

Furniture made of genuine bamboo or of bird's-eye maple or beech turned and carved to resemble bamboo has charmed Americans ever since those days in the late 1880's when the first romantic bamboo imports arrived from the Far East. Because bamboo is easy to keep clean and has an exotic appeal, many American attics have been raided for these treasures.

Regular dusting, plus a wiping now and then with a damp cloth, is all the care bamboo needs. A light waxing will act as a buffer to deter marks and stains and will give an old bamboo piece a fresher look and a more appealingly natural color. Use a natural-base wax, buffing to bring up the original luster. Imitation bamboo of maple or beech requires the same simple care: regular dusting and occasional waxing and polishing to freshen it up.

CANE

Steam-heated houses and apartments are the archenemies of canework, the woven golden bark of the rattan, used by cabinetmakers for seats and backs of chairs, ends of sofas, and panels. During the season when steam heat is used, dampen cane once a month to counteract dryness. With a sponge lightly moistened in warm water, go over the entire canework area. Let dry before using the furniture.

If soil must be removed, wipe canework clean with a sponge dipped in soapy warm water and wrung out nearly dry. Use a mild soap. Rinse with clear warm water and let dry thoroughly.

There are many kits on the market for repairing cane and rush when their fibers give way, but if yours is a valuable antique, have an expert make the repairs. Luckily, many good craftsmen who specialize in this work are still around.

RUSH

Rushwork—woven stalks of rushes or reeds, used primarily for chair seats—is splintered by almost any kind of friction, so avoid washing. Also, moist rushwork is liable to mold. Instead, dust, then wipe clean with a slightly dampened cloth. Once or twice a year coat the rushwork with white shellac. It will dry in twenty to thirty minutes. The shellac will freshen up antique rushwork, protect its stained finish, and smooth out frayed or chipping fibers. It will also hold down loose ends, if you line them up in their rightful places before you shellac. For repairing rushwork see preceding section, "Cane."

MARBLE AND SLATE TABLETOPS

See instructions for the care of these in Chapter 13, "Marble and Slate."

LEATHER

To fend off dryness, which can cause leather upholstery and other leather accessories to crack, peel, and become brittle, maintain room temperature below 70 degrees and humidity around 50 per cent.

If leather passes the wet-finger test, it can be cleaned by regular dusting and by wiping with a barely moist cloth. The test: Touch the leather with a wet finger. If there's no absorption of moisture or darkening of color, proceed to wipe the leather with a cloth dipped in warm, soapy water and wrung almost dry. Rinse with clear water and another clean, wrung-dry cloth. Let dry thoroughly. (Caution: Water on upholstery of vegetable-tanned leather—an early tanning process that used the bark, wood, and other parts of plants and trees—might remove some of the antique leather's natural protective lactates. Vegetable-tanned leather, one expert warns, should be washed only if it is sponged afterward with 10 per cent potassium lactate.) Wax with a natural-base paste wax. Buff with a soft cloth after twenty-four hours.

If leather can't take even this much wetting, dust it with a soft, clean cloth and rub it with another. Then apply a light film of paste wax. Again, buff after twenty-four hours.

WASHING FURNITURE

Although using soap and water on various kinds of fine furniture is frowned upon by some experts (one advises washing only "far gone" pieces or those of questionable value), others contend that nothing freshens a piece better and with less damage than well-controlled washing. Before washing an entire Chippendale highboy or plunging into the intricate carvings of a Victorian half-tester bed, though, experiment on a small, inconspicuous area. If it turns white, forgo this method of cleaning. If no white "bloom" or streaks appear, however, remove the wax with mineral spirits or a synthetic turpentine and proceed at full speed.

Squeeze a sponge almost dry of suds made with a good-quality soap and warm water. The trick is to use as little water as possible and to wash, rinse, and dry a small section before going on to the next. Flush dust out of the crevices of wood carvings with the bristles of a brush covered with an almost dry washcloth. Let the furniture stand twenty-four hours to dry before rewaxing.

INSECT INFESTATION

Tiny mounds of colored powder under an old piece of furniture are telltale signs that insects are zooming in on your antique. The most common raiders are furniture beetles and powder-post beetles, which drill holes you can see better with a magnifying glass than with the naked eye. A third enemy attack may come from termites, which bore from within. Woodworms—beetles' larvae offspring bred in furniture cracks—also bore holes and must be gotten rid of.

Some people prefer to rout these unwelcome visitors with household insecticides sprayed directly into the holes and repeated as needed. Others feel more secure turning over this serious problem to an exterminator. Insecticides may contain solvents of varnish, so be cautious and don't let the spray spatter on a varnished surface.

ROOM CLIMATE

Give your furniture, as you do your paintings, a stable, all-year relative humidity of around 50 per cent and a temperature near 70 to 72 degrees, and you can nip in the bud the deterioration of many fragile antiques. Humidity extremes are more menacing than temperature extremes. If necessary, measure the humidity with a hygrometer. Then control moisture with a humidifier or a dehumidifier.

SUNLIGHT

A picture window may show off your furniture's mellow beauty in the most flattering light, but it also will do the antiques the most harm. Sun-warmed furniture surfaces are at such odds with the cooler atmosphere that the wood can warp, twist, and even crack. Moreover, the mellow color of old wood cannot take much sunlight without fading.

Sunshine contains a good deal of ultraviolet light, the most damaging kind. Protect wooden furniture and other things that might fade—prints, colored fabrics, and so on—by installing windows and window walls of ultraviolet-filtering acrylic plastic, which will reduce sunlight's harmful rays. It is available through established glass-dealers.

NOMADIC ANTIQUES

Household moves from a warm and sunny to a cold and dismal climate or to a house with different heating and air-conditioning systems can have extremely harmful effects on old furniture. The danger of an antique's being ruined by such a move is dramatized by one of today's phenomena: the migrations of America's corporate families. In the decentralization and expansion of industry, many business executives and their families are moved bag and baggage all over this country and abroad. Their antique furniture may be bruised and battered in transit and is apt to deteriorate from a drastic change of locale. Many migrating antique-owners have solved the problem by persuading indulgent relatives and friends to take care of valuable pieces until they are permanently settled.

PACKING AND MOVING ANTIQUES

If you're going to move antiques from one place to another, all artwork and other valuable furnishings should be packed and crated for the journey by a specialized firm of art packers. Decide on a mover with this extra string to his bow after careful choosing (consult your *Yellow Pages*). Choose one who will make a special visit to your home for an inspection of your valuables and who will have paintings, sculpture, and even miniature watercolors picked up and taken to his warehouse for packing, crating, marking for safety warnings, and shipping by air freight. On the same visit he will check out the valuable breakfront or massive dining table that is to be wrapped like Baby Bunting in pads and blankets and shipped by van along with your other household possessions.

Although custom-crating, packing, and sometimes hoisting with a crane run high in cost, their use—closed plywood crates, lavish quantities of glassine or plastic paper, and protective corner pads—inspires confidence and offers peace of mind to owners of irreplaceable treasures, as it often spells the difference between valued pieces arriving intact or in shambles. It is a matter of normal precaution to take out a floater policy to insure these valuables while they are in transit. The same safeguards apply to works of art that you have shipped overseas. Sophisticated movers with branches abroad know all the ins and outs of shipping antiques and will give them the same care for an overseas as for a domestic move.

REUPHOLSTERING

A few years ago if you wanted to reupholster an antique chair or sofa with a fabric of authentic Colonial American design, your quest usually led to a dead end in the American Wing of some museum. Now there are so many historic reproductions on the market that you can take your pick of fabrics, designs, and colors. Replicas range from fabrics used in country homes during the Colonial period to those adorning the elegant rooms of eighteenth-century Newport, Rhode Island. Today's technology not only makes possible distinguished prints, damasks, and brocades but also adds something your ancestors never dreamed of: stain- and dirt-resistant finishes. For suppliers of these fabrics see the listing in "Sources for Materials for the Care of Antiques," page 151.

CHAPTER 8

Glassware

ACCORDING TO LEGEND, the first drinking glass was made by Venus from a bubble of seafoam cut in half. Keeping glassware as pristine as this legendary goblet is no problem with today's know-how and with the countless aids for easy washing, polishing, and curing of "sick" glass.

WASHING

To keep glassware free of dust and grime, a cause of deterioration, take it all from the shelves and wash it two or three times a year. Use warm water and pure soap flakes. Add one-fourth to one-half cup of ammonia to a plastic dishpan of water (a plastic pan will guard against chipping). Dry with two fresh, lint-free paper towels, one to polish the outside, the other to dry the inside simultaneously. Replace with dry towels as soon as the working pair becomes damp.

Routine cleaning of decanters and other narrow-neck containers is made easier if you fill them with warm water, add a few fresh tea leaves, and let soak overnight. Glasses with gilt, silver, and platinum decorations should be ushered briefly in and out of a plastic dishpan filled with warm (never hot) water and pure soap flakes. Do not add ammonia. Rinse and carefully hand-dry with lint-free paper towels.

If you are entranced by the song of champagne bubbles, don't wash champagne glasses with a detergent. Philip Hiaring, author of the syndicated column "The Cheerful Vintner," claims that detergent-washed glasses resist rinsing and that the remaining film spells doom to bubbles. Instead, wash the glasses with salt—half a cupful dissolved in a dishpan of warm water—and rinse with clear warm water. If you insist on using soap, he advises rinsing the glasses under running warm water and placing them right side up on a terrycloth towel to air-dry. Standing glasses will dispel soap smells and, it is said, will keep the flavor of the wine true.

REMOVING STAINS, POLISHING

Glass that has lost its transparency can regain it, at least temporarily, if coated lightly with olive oil. Rub the oil over the glass with a soft woolen rag, polishing until the transparency returns and surplus oil disappears.

For occasional display use a paste-type silver polish on water-stained glass, just as you would use it on a tarnished teapot. It is a spectacular brightener. You must let the polish dry, however, and then rub the glass briskly with a clean, soft rag to make it glow. Wash with warm soapsuds, rinse, and dry.

REMOVING STUBBORN SEDIMENT

If a deposit can't be softened and flushed out of a bottle, cruet, or decanter with warm soapsuds and a bottle brush or a longer prod, such as a flexible twig wrapped in cloth, try another approach. Fill the container with warm water

THIN TWIG

CLOTH

Removing sediment from a decanter with a twig

to which you have added either half a cup of vinegar or two tablespoons of washing soda. Cork and let stand for a couple of days or more. If one solution doesn't work, try the other. Depending on its nature, the crust will usually soften from either the acid or the alkaline soak.

TREATING SICKNESS

When the crystal transparency of a decanter, flask, or bottle has become milky and opaque because of a cloudy haze, the odds are that it has held wine too long or that it has been stored in a damp place and excess humidity has broken down the structure of the glass. Two treatments are commonly prescribed for such glass. First, half fill the container with water or denatured alcohol, add about a cupful of fine clean sand (obtainable from dime stores and other home-aquarium—supply counters), and swirl it around until the glass becomes clear. If this fails, dribble clear, colorless mineral oil down the container's interior sides until they are filmed with oil. This second treatment usually brings only temporary relief for display purposes. To prevent the oil's evaporation put a stopper in loosely. When the oil dries, renew it.

PAMPERING OLD GLASS

For those infrequent occasions when you only want to display antique decanters or bottles fill them with distilled or mineral water, not tap water. If they're to be wine servers, use as briefly as possible. Never store liquids in antique glass containers.

STORING

Keep glassware away from dampness and air-conditioning and heating vents. Glass so exposed will deteriorate. See that your storage cabinet is well ventilated. Never wrap glass in tissue because this will attract moisture. Don't stack; pieces might stick together and be damaged when you try to pull them apart.

RESCUING DAMAGED GLASSWARE

A stem broken off a goblet, a bowl nicked, a vase chipped, and even more serious mishaps aren't quite the Humpty Dumpty disasters they may seem. Specialists in glass repair can use their wheels to graze off scratches and grind nicks and chips down to near invisibility. Snapped-off stems can be reattached or replaced. So visit a glass-repair specialist before you decide to throw out a piece of damaged antique glassware.

CHAPTER 9

Glass Paperweights

GLASS PAPERWEIGHTS are instant magic. When you watch a whirling snowstorm or other fantasy captured in a crystal globe, you enter a make-believe world within a real world. Credit for this escapism in the palm of your hand goes to the Old World art of the glassmaker. Although France is conceded to be the master of it, America also produced, in the early nineteenth century, entrancing handmade glass paperweights. To meet the demand for this enchantment glassmakers in New England and on the eastern seaboard worked night and day floating yellow and pink roses, blue cherries, white cameos, and bits of multicolored canes in small glass spheres.

CLEANING AND POLISHING

Like all other glass, in today's polluted air paperweights acquire a greasy film. Wash it off, as you do from other fine glass, in a plastic dishpan. This greatly reduces the hazards of chipping. (Wipe—don't immerse—paperweights with glued-on bases.) Use suds made of a mild soap and warm

A collection of glass paperweights in a breakfront

(not hot) water. Slippery in your grasp because of their shape, paperweights must be lifted out of soapy dishwater and put into clear, warm rinse-water cautiously. When drying a paperweight, envelop it securely in a clean, rough-textured dish towel.

To put a deluxe sparkle on dulling paperweights use your silver polish occasionally. Rub it on, let it dry, then buff with a soft cotton-flannel cloth until brilliance seems to glance off the glass like rays of light. If the polish is wiped off well, there's no need to wash afterward. The less handling you do, the fewer are the chances for bruises and damaging accidents.

DISPLAYING

The most hazardous place to display paperweights is on a tabletop. So arrayed, they are a temptation to guests who like to pick them up, hold them to the light, and scrutinize their designs. A cabinet is an infinitely safer place for these little gems; there they escape handling, scratches, chipping, wear marks, and perhaps even severe damage from being dropped. If you exhibit them in a lighted vitrine or breakfront cabinet, don't leave the light on too long. Keep doors open for ventilation.

Avoid extremes of heat and cold. Paperweights, like other fine glass, are also sensitive to dampness. Keep humidity in the room between 60 and 65 per cent.

REPAIRING

Much can be done by a glass cutter or glass polisher who specializes in the repair of paperweights. He can grind, smooth, and polish away scratches and minor fractures. Major fractures—the cracks that go all the way through a globe—can often be concealed. He can polish a collector's treasure so that it recaptures its original luster, and he can reshape a weight by recutting damaged facets. Sometimes a cracked paperweight can be redesigned so that this liability is transformed into an asset.

CHAPTER 10

Ivory and Bone

THE ARTIST'S SKILL that converted gleaming, finely grained tusks of African elephants and other large mammals into objects of irresistible charm—including watercolor portraits the size of a locket—makes old ivories intriguing treasures. Figurines, richly carved coffers, doughty chessmen on ivory chessboards, jewel-like handles of knightly daggers and swords, all enchant the amateur collector.

CLEANING AND CARE

The simple rules for the care of ivory also apply to bone. Both dentine substances are toothlike in structure and made up of layers. If allowed to get too wet, the layers will separate and, like wood, swell unevenly, warp, and crack. Bone, not as fragile as ivory and of firmer texture, carves well and can take a wetting if you dry it immediately.

To clean ivory use a damp sponge with a mild soap, rinse with clear tepid water, and dry immediately with a soft nonabrasive cloth (the Brooklyn Museum likes to use the soft cotton jersey that T-shirts are made of). Some proud ivory-owners, after cleaning a piece, rub on the merest hint of almond oil to heighten the luster.

Provide a dry room-climate for both ivory and bone. Dampness can make the layers separate. Strong sunlight and heat are just as damaging; they cause discoloration and flaking.

A gradual deepening of color, from creamy whiteness to soft golden-yellow, is part of the aging process. This deeper color is the mature bloom, or patina. No connoisseur finds it displeasing, especially when he learns that patinated carvings have greater value. Yellowing ivory, however, can be bleached by an expert ivory-restorer if this is desired. Piano keys are frequently removed and whitened at the factory of their origin, but since the keys lose their whiteness during a natural cycle of deepening color, bleaching would seem to be a waste of time and money.

Ivory- or Bone-Handled Knives

Wash each knife separately, and *not* in the dishpan. Nor should knives be entrusted to a dishwasher. As noted above, wetness is the enemy, so wash by hand, confining water to the blade.

For special cleaning of the handles ingenious souls dampen a dishcloth with a little kerosene and rub off stains. Afterward, rinse with a cloth or sponge dipped in hot water and wrung out. Drying quickly is important.

HALTING THE CRACKING OF IVORY

Figurines and carvings long exposed to a dry atmosphere often develop cracks, but they can be controlled. Ivory fibers are living things, and they can be kept from separating by using a liquid furniture wax to bind them together.

Before attempting to fill the cleavage in a figurine or carving with as much wax as it will take without spilling over, tape all around the crack with masking tape so that wax will flow into the opening and not onto ivory surfaces. If any wax goes astray, wipe it off. For filling a crack a pointed artist's brush, similar to one a watercolorist uses, is the best kind of applicator.

Allow the wax from one to two days to dry and then remove masking tape. This treatment should halt cracking for six months to a year. When cracking threatens again, renew the treatment.

PRESERVING WATERCOLOR MINIATURES

The care of these tiny portraits on ivory can be summed up in three words: Don't touch them! A former art-gallery director who feels strongly about this has a rigid set of rules: Don't try to clean these miniatures, no matter how dusty or dirty they get, even when they're sealed under glass. Don't remove them from their frames. If a minature must be opened, call in an expert. (Ask your museum to recommend a reputable specialist.)

To avoid strong light hang ivory miniatures in a dark corner, free from dampness, open fires, and radiators. When these perishable beauties are not being displayed, keep them in a covered receptacle.

CHAPTER 11

Iron

WE HAVE INHERITED from the mid-nineteenth century an almost limitless variety of elegant and utilitarian iron objects for the home, garden, and public places. They embrace everything from morning-glory settees that are a bower of blooms fit for Titania to radiator covers as fragile looking as *point-Venise* lace.

ROUTING RUST

As strong and enduring as iron is, nearly all the old pieces that have been handed down bring with them a legacy of rust. This is less likely to be the burden of wrought iron, which was tempered with oil during manufacture.

To defeat rust, or ferric hydroxide—formed by water's combining with iron—arm yourself with kerosene, a wire brush with a long, curved handle, and a mountainous heap of old rags (to be disposed of as fast as they become oily to avoid the dangers of spontaneous combustion. To get rid of these oily rags safely, stuff them into a double plastic bag and wrap the ends of the bags with twists of household wire to make them airtight. Put bags in a garbage can with a closed lid for regular household disposal.)

After applying kerosene to a piece of iron, let it stay until it flows under the rust so you can lift the rust off with your wire brush. You'll need, however, to scrape persistently to clean off rust uniformly from the entire surface. Old scales, chips, and every stubborn spot must yield. Sometimes it may be necessary to chip some of the rust loose by chiseling or tapping with a small hammer.

Creating a No-Rust Climate

To keep iron rust-free, protect it from dampness. If necessary, plug in an electric dehumidifier to dry out the room.

NEW PAINT FOR OLD IRON

When the iron is clean, apply a primer coat of red lead to seal the surface. Let this dry thoroughly—twenty-four hours or longer—before you paint. The new aerosol paints, available at hardware and paint-supply stores, are easier to apply and produce smoother results than do brush-on paints. Spray paints are obtainable in mat or gloss finishes. They come in colors that duplicate those of antique iron chandeliers, candelabra, Betty lamps, and furniture: inky black, gunmetal, or whatever is needed. Caution: Aerosol paints should not be used indoors.

OUTDOOR FURNITURE

To remove rust and to paint an antique garden bench, a weathervane, or the hardware on shutters use the above

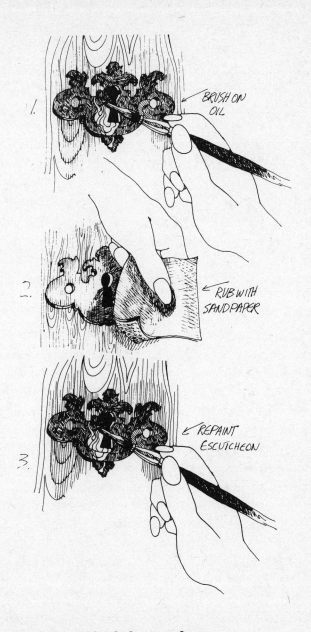

1. BRUSH ON OIL

2. RUB WITH SANDPAPER

3. REPAINT ESCUTCHEON

Restoring rust-bound keyhole escutcheon

technique but with a little less finesse. As long as paint on outdoor iron forms a solid covering, there's no danger of further rust. If water breaks through the paint barrier, merely repainting where the break occurred will protect the entire piece.

RESTORING ANTIQUE HARDWARE

When iron hinges, locks, bolts, and keyhole escutcheons on antique furniture become so rusted that they mar the piece or cease to be functional, give them the following treatment:

First, apply a lubricating oil. Use a small brush and take care not to let oil overflow onto the wood. Leave the oil on overnight. Next day rub it off with a cloth.

Sand off the loosened rust with coarse sandpaper or chip it off with a wire brush, depending upon the hardware's fragility. Clean the hardware with a kerosene rag, and if the work is outdoors, leave the oil on, rough-brushing until almost dry to remove loose rust particles. Then apply primer and paint. If the work is indoors, wipe the kerosene off with a dry rag and rub the hardware clean with a cloth moistened with turpentine. Apply a red-lead primer coat. Then with a paint duplicating the color and mat or gloss of the old finish, repaint. When you have had to replace a broken or missing hinge, use paint matching the other hardware on the furniture.

If removing a broken hinge is difficult because of rust-bound screws, put a drop of "liquid wrench" lubricating oil on each. Tap the screws with a hammer to make oil flow into the cavities. Wait an hour or so for screws to loosen up, then extract them.

CHAPTER 12

Lead Sculpture

ALTHOUGH LEAD SCULPTURES are too rustic and too lacking in fine detail to become indoor art objects, they take to garden niches and trompe-l'oeil vistas as naturally as moss takes to trees. When such sculptures and classic urns, vases, sundials, and fountains graced our nineteenth-century gardens, this country was producing a third of the world's output of lead. Instead of being harmed by weather, lead is little affected by it. The metal acquires a thin coating of oxide, which prevents further corrosion. Turning white with irregular streaking, this carbonate of lead deposit is a mark of patination which connoisseurs find extremely beautiful in the ambience of a garden's greenery.

DON'T CLEAN IT

The older and dirtier lead sculptures and other garden ornaments become, the better they usually look. So don't try to clean them and risk robbing them of their natural patina. Just protect them from wind and sand; a soft metal, lead may lose detail when cut by wind-blown sand and other debris.

REFURBISHING

If lead sculpture eventually deteriorates badly and has no patina to redeem it, a coat of paint will revitalize it. Before painting, sand it with emery paper or emery cloth. Use a lead-base paint of the same bluish-gray color the sculpture had when it was cast.

You can also restore metallic luster to an old neglected piece by coating it with clear lacquer. This will give a bronze-type gloss to a muscular gladiator or to an engraved urn, the sentimental grave marker for a pet.

CHAPTER 13

Marble and Slate

FROM THE SLAB TOP on the walnut washstand to Diana hiding in a boxwood niche, marble has been a hallmark of luxury in this country since the nineteenth century. Slate, a modest foil to the assertive marble, played a supporting role during the marble-top and -statuary era. Slate's matlike finish and dark, understated chic have made it a favorite of many collectors today, however.

MARBLE

Marble—hard limestone that can be highly polished— seems to have everything going for it. It is exotically colored, it has fantastic patterns, and when it is pure white, it is hauntingly beautiful. Its porosity makes it highly vulnerable to staining, however.

CLEANING

Dust is a carrier of soot and iron particles, both stainers of fine marble. Remove these, along with deposits from fumes and smoke in the atmosphere, by daily dusting of your indoor marble pieces with a feather duster or a soft-bristled brush. Never use a cloth that can grind in dust.

Experts believe that some marble sculpture that has become dirty should remain that way. Washing it would destroy its delicate contrasts of highlights and shadows. Don't wash old marble with a weathered look that seems to become warmer in tone and more translucent with the years. Give it the least possible cleaning.

Polished white and light-colored marbles are a risk to wash and should be cautiously tested on an inconspicuous area before an allover wetting. To test, experiment with the suds of a mild soap and warm distilled water. Apply with a soft white rag, rinse with a cloth wrung out almost dry in clear water, and dry quickly with a fresh cloth. If the response is favorable, dust the marble thoroughly, then wash, rinse, and dry a small patch before going on to the next. White marble is highly susceptible to staining by damp colored bath towels, washcloths, and soap. Don't subject it to contact with these bathroom accessories.

There are stain removers on the market, but the best way to cope with stains is to prevent them. Have, as one wary hostess advises, a stack of coasters to forestall rings made by perspiring glasses. Removing stains is epecially difficult because of their wandering-gypsy habit of penetrating the porous stone far from where a spill occurred. Don't let spilled liquid that might stain remain any longer than it takes to mop it up. If necessary, apply then and there a first-aid stain remover from your household kit.

Commercial marble polishes are available. Many devout fanciers, however, use instead a dusting of talcum powder rubbed over the surface with a soft cloth until a gleam appears.

Cleaning outdoor marbles

Outdoor Marbles

As you do with indoor marbles, dust outdoor sculpture and garden furniture before washing. Then wash with mild soap and distilled water mixed with a little ammonia. Work the soap into a stiff lather. With a soft-bristled brush, begin at the top of the piece and wash a small patch of marble at a time, drying it with a soft, clean rag. Then proceed to the next patch. Try to wash more with the lather than with the water; otherwise, the soiled water can stream down over the unwashed area and make cleaning harder. When the entire piece has been washed, rinse off all soap with the garden hose or a pail of water. Then dry thoroughly with a huge supply of soft, clean cloths.

Unpolished Marble Floors

When an old floor stubbornly resists regular cleaning, try the following method, recommended by the Vermont Marble Company, of Proctor, Vermont, one of the country's largest quarriers. Fill a shaker can with a nonabrasive detergent. Wet the floor with clean water. Then sprinkle the detergent on very sparingly and work up a lather with a flexible floor brush or a mop. So the mop's metal frame won't scrape the floor, tie a towel around any part that drags. Scrub a patch of floor, remove the soiled water, and rinse before going on to the next area. Use a clean mop and a pail of fresh water for the cleanup. If the dried floor is streaked with white powder, either you have been too lavish with the detergent or the floor was not properly rinsed.

SLATE

Smooth as wet silk and most familiar when it's a dark bluish gray or black, sparkling with mica, slate has many household applications. Lauded for its strength, durability, slight water absorption, and a habit of drying quickly, it is best used as floor tiles and stair treads.

CLEANING

One owner of antique tiles in mint condition has cleaned them for years by dry mopping one day, damp mopping the next. You can follow her mopping routine; for good measure, also scrub once a week with soap and water. Because some tile colors have a tendency to fade, avoid using strong scouring powders or bleaches, especially on black slate. One-half cup of soap flakes dissolved in one or two gallons of hot water makes a mild cleaning solution. If there are grease spots, add a little ammonia to the water and use a brush. Use two cotton mops: one to scrub with and a fresh one for rinsing with cold water.

To bring up a low-key luster use a self-polishing floor wax, lightly buffed, or lemon oil. Moisten a mop with the oil and lightly rub it over the slate surfaces. Let the oil set for two or three hours. A clean, dry mop vigorously applied or a weighted buffer can also be used to heighten slate's inherent sparkle.

BEAUTY TREATMENT

Slate fireplace hearths and facings, pull-out leaves in writing desks, and small-to-massive tabletops are instantly transformed from nondescript gray to lustrous granite black by a beauty treatment with lemon oil. Be generous with it; leave it on for a few minutes, then wipe it off with a soft cotton cloth. Lemon oil also minimizes scratches and rings from water or liquor glasses.

CHAPTER 14

Music Boxes

WHETHER THEY ARE simple miniatures that play lilting tunes on a few tiny bells, or large instruments in exotic wood cabinets lavish with multicolored inlays, music boxes have held audiences in thrall through the centuries. Peasant and prince, student and maestro, child and adult, have tapped their feet to the music. Composers of the stature of Joseph Haydn and Wolfgang Amadeus Mozart wrote music for them. Ludwig van Beethoven's favorite tune was Luigi Cherubini's overture to *Médée* as played on a music box in a Viennese café. Music boxes are as popular with collectors today as they were in the eighteenth century.

PLACING THIS TREASURE

Don't expose a music box to direct sunlight, and keep it at a safe distance from radiators and fireplaces. Heat will cause the wooden case to crack and warp and the inlays to pop out. In many music boxes, especially the Swiss-made, heat will cause the cementlike substance to pull away from the cylinder, causing hollow sounds when the music is playing. Dampness, also an enemy, should be controlled by installing a dehumidifier in the room.

OILING THE MECHANISM

Use watch-lubricating oil, available at watch-repair and jewelry shops, to oil the mechanism of your music box. To apply the smallest amount possible dip the end of a toothpick into the bottle, shake off the drop, and put what oil is left on a bearing. Repeat for each bearing. Do this every few months. Caution: Limiting lubricating oil to an infinitesimal amount can't be overemphasized; otherwise, dust, attracted to the oiled parts, will stick. Also, a very small amount of Vaseline rubbed on the edge of a stiff piece of paper or cardboard and passed over the cylinder pins while the music is playing will help keep the mechanism properly lubricated.

HANDLING

After playing your music box, always be sure that a tune has ended and the lever is on "stop." Do not hold the box on its side unless the lever is on "stop" and the tune has ended. The parts disengaged during playing can shift and damage the points on the teeth.

Keep the spring just slightly wound at all times. This is especially important when you are making a household move or shipping the music box. It prevents the spring from disconnecting in the spring barrel. In packing the music box for shipping, lightly wedge a small piece of tissue in the governor (the box's mechanical "brain") and place a cork between the spring barrel and cylinder to prevent shifting.

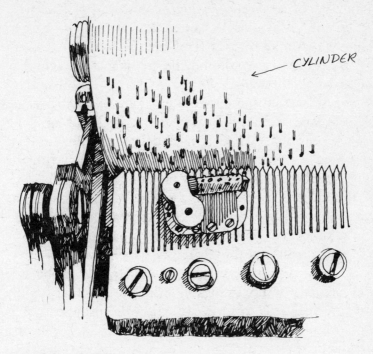

CYLINDER

Music-box insides

SERVICING

Being checked and properly attended to by a qualified specialist *once*—the best time is when you acquire it—will give your music box immunity from repairs for many years. So claims Rita Ford, a New York dealer and owner of one of the country's most distinctive collections of rare antique music boxes.

One sign that a box is in trouble and may need servicing, says Mrs. Ford, is a slowing down of pace. Speed is lost, and no amount of winding brings it back. The trouble may be caused by a common malfunction. The works may be gummed up by an accumulation of dust and dirt. Letting the machine go too long without servicing can cause this trouble, which may be averted if the mechanisms are kept clean, gears are inspected, and the box is given a complete —not a partial—servicing.

A spring that is beginning to break may be another cause of slowed pace. A music-box spring can start tearing like a spring in a watch. When a mechanism as strategic as a spring breaks, it causes other parts to give way, with the result that extensive repairs may be required.

If the cylinder revolves too fast—in other words, if the movement goes berserk—it may be due to a spindle that has begun to crack. A spindle is an essential part of the "governor," which controls the speed at which the music box plays. When the spindle breaks, it activates the spring into unwinding very fast, causing the cylinder to rotate rapidly out of control. This in turn can cause the projecting pins on the cylinder to become bent or torn off. These pins are positioned so that as the cylinder revolves, they hit the teeth of a steel comb. Each tooth of the comb has a point that, when it strikes the pins on the cylinder revolving at an accelerated speed, can be broken (the teeth and/or the points), and the pins on the cylinder can become badly damaged. Unless caught in time, this trouble may mean a costly restoration.

CHAPTER 15

Papier-mâché

D<small>URING THE VICTORIAN ERA</small> American artists and craftsmen created a diversity of papier-mâché trays, tea caddies, lap desks, and even furniture, bequeathing to us a legacy of brilliant innovations in decorative objects of "chewed paper." Mechanically macerated paper pulp mixed with sizing and hardened into molded forms produced accessories that cast a radiance over the entire home. Their colorful character was enhanced by embellishments of tortoiseshell, mother-of-pearl, gold leaf, and sometimes flower, landscape, and portrait paintings.

RULES OF CARE

Although papier-mâché pieces often boast as many as sixty layers of lacquer or varnish and are hard enough to be sawed in two, they are vulnerable to extreme drying conditions, to the effects of moisture, and to paper-devouring insects, especially silverfish, when their surface cracks or breaks. Paradichlorobenzene crystals—a mild insecticide—laid between tissues in lap-desk drawers, sprinkled into box linings, placed inside clock cases and on storage shelves, can offer protection for papier-mâché pieces. At the end of six months fumes from these crystals will have evaporated, and they should be renewed. This insecticide must never be applied directly to painted decorations, as it can dissolve certain types of lacquer used in painting scenery or flowers on papier-mâché articles. If objects are valuable, ask the paper conservator of your museum to prescribe the best care.

Don't expose papier-mâché to direct sunlight or place it near hot or cold vents. Never put hot food or drinks on a papier-mâché tray. Be careful not to spill either hot or cold liquids on it. Dust papier-mâché frequently with a soft, clean cloth, free of abrasives, so knife-sharp particles won't be ground into the varnish.

The problem in cleaning is to lift the film of soil from ornate works without damaging their luster or decorations. The best and safest way is to use a furniture cream that both cleans and polishes. Apply it sparingly and quickly with a clean, dry, soft cloth; wipe it off in circular motions with a follow-up cloth. As with Oriental lacquer, you can't clean papier-mâché with a damp cloth without risking damage. If moisture penetrates to the paper foundation and makes it swell or crack, the surface lacquer will be rejected or will peel. The foundation of papier-mâché is even more vulnerable to moisture damage than plain wood- or metal-based articles.

When metal hardware on papier-mâché develops tarnish, remove it with a cleaning cloth impregnated with metal polish. This eliminates smeary cream run-overs. Pack tissue around handles, hinges, and locks to isolate smudges. They can be instantly wiped off with a soft, clean, dry cloth. Polish the hardware with a second clean cloth.

Never try your hand at touch-ups. If a tree is fading out

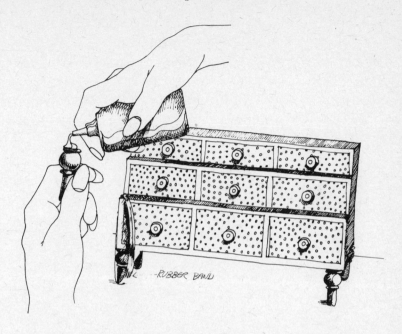

RUBBER BAND

Mending a papier-mâché jewelry box

of a painted scene or a face has lost a feature, be happy with the less-than-pristine glory of a charming old piece. If you feel the piece must be restored, let a professional do it.

Too much cannot be said about the bad effects of a wax buildup on the surface of papier-mâché. Although one coating can work wonders in restoring luster, multiple layers not only dull the lacquer but also obscure the decorations. To remove this heavy coating use the furniture cream described above.

DO-IT-YOURSELF MENDING

To make a repair of a simple nature on a piece that is not valuable enough for professional care—a jewelry box with a detached leg, the lid of a game box split in half—use one of the white household glues. (Never use a glue with a lacquer base—one that smells strongly of nail polish.) Apply the white glue sparingly to the two parts to be cemented together. Clamp them tightly in place with rubber bands. Leave them for twelve hours to dry. Please don't try to mend any piece of value.

CHAPTER 16

Pewter

WHEN PEWTER REPLACED wooden bowls, platters, tankards, and trenchers on the tables of our Pilgrim ancestors, this was eloquent proof of the rapidly rising standard of Colonial living. As the demand for pewter tableware grew, skilled metalworkers migrated to the Colonies from England and the Continent to set up shop. They created many of the simple, classic pieces of pewter which collectors value today.

Much fine early-American pewter was lost to posterity because it was melted down to make bullets. Also, families traded off unneeded pieces to itinerant peddlers who in turn passed them on to metalsmiths. The smiths converted them into objects of inferior quality and design.

CARE AND UPKEEP

Because pewter is essentially a soft metal—an alloy of tin and lead or of tin and copper, with other metals some-times added—be careful not to batter it around. Don't take it too close to the open flames of a stove, hearth, or burning

PEWTER
TEAPOT

Cleaning pewter

candle. Pewterers today are kept busy filling burned holes in antique ware with melted-down scraps.

Wear cotton gloves when you polish pewter. Fingerprints can cause tarnish that has to be coped with all over again. Don't polish too vigorously or use a harsh cleaner. A commercial foaming polish that puts a sheen on silver without scratching it will do as much for pewter. The tendency to clean blackened pewter with an abrasive presents the ever-present danger of cutting deep into the metal. The judicious use of fine steel wool (000 grade) dipped into a little olive oil will often unleash the grip of stubborn spots without leaving any scratches. Once pewter is cleaned, a polished sheen can be renewed from time to time with a woolen rag dipped in olive oil.

In deference to pewter's patina—the oxidized shadow effects that make ornamental relief stand out—polish only the high, silvery planes. No part of pewter, however, should look overbright. Pewter should never be chemically dipped (to remove tarnish by chemical solvents) or professionally buffed. Never store old pewter in drawers or cupboards of oak, a wood that releases volatile tannic acid, which can damage objects containing lead.

CHAPTER **17**

Porcelain and Earthenware

AMERICAN-MADE HARD-FIRED PORCELAIN, so sheer and translucent that a candle flame will shine through it, had tough competition at the Philadelphia Centennial in 1876, our one-hundredth birthday party. Imports from England, France, China, and other Far Eastern countries strutted like drum majors while dishes of native china were sold with giveaway cans of baking powder. Today collectors and museums highly prize native porcelain and make much of the smashing patterns that decorate brilliantly glazed earthenware.

CLEANING

Nonabsorbent, nonporous, hard-fired porcelain made from fine clays is the easiest of all china to clean. Menacing it is scalding hot water, which can cause a fine network of cracks in the glaze, called crazing. Water comfortably hot for your hands and a mild soap should be used. So should a plastic dishpan to guard against chipping. Never use a dishwasher. Immediately after use, dishes should be washed, rinsed in clean hot water, and thoroughly dried. If food is left too long in earthenware, which is porous, liquids will seep through the glaze and sink in, staining the dishes.

Tea and coffee rings and other stubborn discolorations can be rubbed off cups and saucers with baking soda moistened with a little water. Future stains can be prevented by instant rinsing after using. Mineral rings that build up on porcelain and earthenware vases frequently can be rubbed off with a damp cloth dipped in salt. A dab of damp salt can be tried on many kinds of stains, including tannic acid, on porcelain.

China should not stand in dishwater if there are gilt bandings and other decorations which might be damaged by soaking. Gilded beauties should be washed with Ivory Liquid, which won't harm the gold. If the gold burnishes, you can remove the undesirable brown color by rubbing it with your thumb. China with raised hand-painted enamel motifs and other decorations in relief should never be carelessly piled at dishwashing time. Separate it from other dishes and gently scrub each piece with the soapy bristles of a soft brush.

Don't immerse in dishwater porcelain art-pieces mounted on metal bases or those having bands, prongs, or other metal decorations. First, clean the metal as you would any pewter, brass, or copper. Rinse off the polish, concentrating on removing run-over smears. With a cloth dipped in warm soapsuds, clean the porcelain. Then wring the cloth out in clear water and use it to rinse the porcelain.

Some collectors report good results in cleaning porcelain and earthenware with dirt-filled cracks in the glaze. Their simple trick is to rub the cracks with damp salt applied with a cotton pad. One collector claims near-magical success with a treasured tureen. Experts are inclined to tell you to minimize the appearance of the dirt in cracks by bleaching the soil. They use as a bleaching agent hydrogen peroxide of

A teapot being poulticed

3 per cent strength, which may be increased if the reaction of the porcelain shows tolerance. Wearing rubber gloves and being sure to protect your eyes, saturate a cotton pad, place it poultice fashion over the crack, and tie or tape it to the china. Keep the pad wet. Lift the pad now and then to check progress. From one to three days may be needed for the bleach to work. If the solution is too strong or is left on too long, it can damage the glaze. Such damage would make the surface look like very fine sandpaper.

STORING DISHES

Padded packing paper is the best cushion to use between plates. Ask the china shops. Also, more handles break when cups hang than when they nest on shelves, stacked in individual cases. Spout-covers of padded paper will guard teapots and coffeepots against crashing encounters on the storage shelf. Finial-crested lids of sugar bowls and jam pots should be turned upside down.

MENDING BROKEN CHINA

Turn repairs over to a skilled ceramist, not to a repairman who will merely cement pieces together. The expert restorer will seal broken edges with special china adhesive and refire the piece in a kiln after each fragment is back in place. He will know what temperature to use without endangering the glaze or the color of the decoration. He will also know whether or not the piece can be refired. Missing parts can be rebuilt, and marred finishes can be retouched.

CHAPTER *18*

Rugs

THE MOST TYPICAL floor coverings in Colonial American homes were hooked and braided rugs. The braided rug is indigenous. The hooked rug crossed the border into New England from French Canada, and every American woman who could collect a bag of bright yarn and could push a hook promptly made one. Many women still do. By 1700, however, Oriental rugs from the Near East were rolling down ships' gangplanks and bedecking well-to-do American homes. You see such rugs on the elegant floors of museums' American Wings, but as old prints bear proof, these rich Oriental "carpitts"—Ushakhs, Bergamas, and Ghiordes— were more often used as table-covers than as floor-coverings.

HOOKED AND BRAIDED RUGS

CLEANING

The processes of cleaning hooked and braided rugs are almost exactly the same. Vacuum both sides of the rug, using a light-duty vacuum with a rug-and-floor–nozzle attachment. In the case of a round or oval braided rug, follow the direction of the braiding.

To wash use soap flakes mixed with lukewarm water (in a ratio of three tablespoons to one gallon) and a dash of Clorox. With an eggbeater, whip the solution until a stiff foam is formed. Color-test by dipping a sponge into the foam and rubbing a small area of the rug's *underside*. Let the foam dry. If colors run, apply the solution without Clorox for a second test. If colors still run, resign yourself to sending your rug to the dry cleaner.

If, however, the color-testing is successful, sponge the foam on the rug and rub it in lightly. Again, follow direction of braiding for a braided rug. For a hooked rug apply with a circular motion. Lay the rug flat on the floor or on a table to dry. When it is dry, vacuum as you did to remove soil.

Latex Backing

To save an old hooked rug from going to pieces give it a liquid-latex backing. (When myriad breaks in the burlap foundation occur, a hooked rug is beginning to deteriorate completely.) Apply the latex—which you can order from a Sears, Roebuck catalog—with a brush or spatula, spreading it evenly all over the burlap. Leave it overnight to dry.

For a rug that is in a worse state of deterioration you can hold it together better by mounting it on a linen or canvas back. Cut the fabric to fit the rug, allowing for a margin. Then douse latex all over the back of the rug and slap the fabric firmly into the liquid. Let it dry overnight. The next day trim the margin. Remember in making the above repairs that it will be practically impossible ever to mend the rug again.

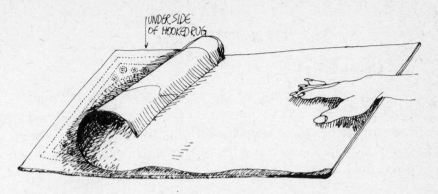

UNDER SIDE
OF HOOKED RUG

Mounting a rug

BINDING THE EDGES

When burlap deteriorates, the edges go first. So if they are frayed, bind the rug. Use a 1½-inch rug-binding and a carpet needle.

OTHER TIPS ON MAINTENANCE

Fill in small holes of a hooked rug before they grow into big ones. Match the yarn in weight and color and use a carpet needle to pull the wool through from front to back. Make loops about 2½ inches high. When the gap is no longer visible, clip the yarn to conform to the height of the pile. Don't try to yank out sprouting ends of yarn. Trim with scissors.

If the plaited rag strips of a braided rug break loose, sew them fast. Roll up a hooked rug top-side out so as not to stretch the burlap. Don't shake or beat a burlap-backed rug. Put glides on furniture legs so they won't crush the pile of a hooked rug. Give hooked and braided rugs outdoor airings often, preferably on cloudy days.

ORIENTAL RUGS

CLEANING

Using *only* a suction-type vacuum cleaner, follow the pile; don't go against it. Vacuum out all particles of grit that can cut strands of wool, and clip off clumps of pile. Vacuum Orientals once a week and have an expert clean and moth-proof them once a year.

OTHER TIPS ON MAINTENANCE

Watch for wear and tear under chairs where TV action is and shift rug positions often. Keep a wary eye out for children's dirty shoes. To keep out embedded grit, which takes professional cleaning to remove, natives of Oriental countries remove their shoes and put on slippers when entering a house. Have holes, loose bindings, worn-down tuft, and other small damaged areas mended before the damage increases.

CHAPTER 19

Silver

AMERICAN WOMEN have a long-standing affinity for old silver, which so brightly illumines their environment, has traditionally decorated their homes, is a rich garnish for their tables, and offers them unlimited opportunities to indulge in romantic illusions.

BATTLING TARNISH

The way to keep old silver flatware and hollow ware safe from tarnish is to guard it against sulphur contaminants. These include sulphides in a city's atmosphere as well as in certain types of water-base paint containing casein, cabinets with rubber seals, rubber-backed mats, and rubber bands. Ordinary rubber bands, so easy to reach for and use to bind together a set of spoons, knives, or forks, can wreak havoc with silver.

You can prevent tarnish by making your silver chest, cabinet drawers, and entire storage chests safe refuges from silver sulphides. Lining these areas throughout with a commercially impregnated cotton-flannel cloth may hold off tarnish for weeks.

Silver serving dishes can be blackened by holding food too long and may then need machine-polishing, an abrasive process that removes some of the silver. Silver bowls and vases not protected with glass liners will suffer the same contamination from flowers left in them to wither and die.

POLISHING

Cleaning off tarnish is mostly a matter of using an efficient polish that doesn't scratch. Silver is highly vulnerable to abrasive treatment. Harsh-bristled brushes can do untold damage to the patina. A commercial foaming polish, almost as nonabrasive in action as a kitten lapping up cream, keeps Buckingham Palace's fabulous collection of silver bright and guards the luster on the U.S. State Department's collection of American silver antiques.

To apply polish use a sponge wrung out of warm water. Work up a lather all over the silver piece. Rinse under running water and dry with a soft dry cloth. Rub old Sheffield plate lightly, or you'll uncover unsightly spots of black base-metal. Because silver plate is softer than sterling, it calls for a lighter touch.

Don't attack channels of ornamental patterns with such vigor that these recessed areas are blanched by deoxidizing. Don't use chemical dips (solvents) that remove the shadowy ornamentation many silver designs owe to oxidation.

In general, wash off polish with warm water and pure soap and rinse well. Because of new tarnish preventatives, however, it is well to follow instructions on the bottle as to whether or not you should wash off the polish. Today's heavily chlorinated water can discolor silver and other metals, and air drying can cause water-spotting, so dry silver instantly and thoroughly with a soft towel. Some experts say that silver should be polished but never professionally buffed, which can remove the patina.

ROUTINE CLEANING

All silver—especially knives—should be washed right after use. Stainless-steel blades can be pitted by salt left on them too long; however, a jeweler can remove pit marks with a buffing wheel. If you find brown stains on your silver, switch to another detergent. Try enough brands to find one that suits your silver.

Silver thrives with everyday use, developing a patina of microscopic lines and a soft richness of color. If you use your silver frequently, you shouldn't have to polish it more than twice a year.

CHAPTER 20

Textiles

Leaving a romantic abode in attic trunks, heirloom quilts, puffs, and bed curtains benefit from technology's rapid advances in climate, pest, and pollution control, space logistics, and storage innovations—all of which outwit time.

ROOM CLIMATE

Sun-fading of textiles is highly visible, but what you can't readily see sunlight do is weaken and destroy the fabric threads. This destruction is intensified if textiles are used or stored in a damp place. An ideal climate offers them a temperature between 60 and 65 degrees and a constant relative humidity of about 50 per cent. Both room and storage closets should be well ventilated even if you have to install fans. Storage areas must under no condition be exposed to ultraviolet light.

FOLDING

This is another nemesis of textiles, yet in today's space squeeze they must submit to it. Many of the hazards of creasing can be avoided by making as few folds as possible and by changing the folds frequently—from thirds to quarters, for example, and then in reverse.

Roll (rather than fold) table linens on poles like those used in deluxe hand laundries. Pole rolling is especially a boon for linen. Flax is so susceptible to abrasion that creasing has been known to cut linen as sharply as would a razor blade. Small linen tablecloths, mats, and napkins too large to be stored flat can be rolled in cardboard tubes. Claiming untenanted corners of closets, such rolls can relieve the burden of crowded cabinet drawers.

KEEPING UNDER GLASS

It's safe to keep valuable hand-embroidered cottons, linens, or silk hangings under glass, but be sure the glass doesn't rest on the embroidery. For protection against sulphur dioxide, a new urban foe of fragile old fabrics, seal the heirloom against dust and air. Hang it on a wall far from a barrage of sunlight.

Your children's baptismal dresses, caps, and other memorable clothing, so delicate they almost defy handling, can be laundered and treated for preservation by specialized hand laundries. In the meantime they can be sophisticated wall decorations if properly mounted and framed under light-deflecting glass in a mothproof shadow box. Actress Mary Martin has used this charming device to preserve two

A child's dress preserved in a shadow box

of her daughter's dresses. One is Heller's christening robe of lawn and lace; the other is a dress she wore as a four-year-old when, like the pussycat in the nursery rhyme, she went to see the British queen.

INSECTS

The first line of defense against insect damage is scrupulous cleanliness. Young clothes moths don't feed on fabric. They subsist entirely, even for their daily vitamins, on food spots and stains. Therefore, the danger of moths attacking a clean textile is almost zero, but you can't be too careful. Carpet beetles will feed on fibers of even clean woolens, so it's best to provide storage protection.

When not in use, textiles can be kept safe from pests by

wrapping them in polyethylene bags fortified with mothball crystals (naphthalene) or paradichlorobenzene (camphor) crystals. Sprinkle one tablespoon of crystals in the folds of a quilt. If the bag is made airtight so fumes can't escape, vapors are maintained inside it at a high level. This protection will be effective for two years.

These crystals can also be sprinkled between folds of fabric and over tissue paper layered between textiles stored in chest drawers, cabinets, and armoires. Although crystals thus used are less effective—their fumes last about six months —they can be renewed when they have evaporated. If crystals are placed in an open dish in the upper part of a cabinet, the vapor, being heavier than air, will mix with the atmosphere below.

Effective only for local treatment of textiles in use—a large wall-hanging or a window wall of curtains—where insects are seen or otherwise known to be present is a spray of pyrethrum, a fungicide extracted from the chrysanthemum plant. This will immediately destroy infestation, but only in the area sprayed. It will not be effective in these concentrated spurts for a period longer than forty-eight hours. Since pyrethrum has an oil base, be sure to read the label's directions about safeguards against staining. A direct spray such as this should not be used on valuable hangings. The problem should be turned over to a professional.

For general protection insecticides should be applied to textiles only after they have been dry-cleaned or washed. Brushing, no matter how thorough, is usually not enough.

MOLD

The presence of mold—parasitic fungi that cause mildew —is announced by furry white and discolored patches. They attach themselves, along with a musty odor, to textiles, leather, paper, and other materials. Discovered on a textile, molds are a warning that it should be washed or dry-cleaned and then moved to dry surroundings.

Paradichlorobenzene crystals, used as described above for destroying moths and carpet beetles, will inhibit growth of mold on stored textiles. Effective in routing mold and musty odors from storage rooms is the use of an electric heater plugged in now and then to dispel dampness. Used for an occasional brief spell, a heater can also help to reduce humidity in a hall or foyer where textile decorations hang.

WASHING HEIRLOOM FABRICS

Experts have two methods for safely washing fragile textiles. Step by step, here are those methods for cleaning priceless cotton and linen heirlooms.

FIRST METHOD

If you shield your fabrics from their own weight when water-soaked –they are three times heavier wet than dry– and from your own hands, you can without damage float decades of grime out of the yellowing heirlooms you find in attic trunks. There are a few super laundries, usually hidden in the shadows of great museums and historical houses, to which curators turn for restorations. Following the method these laundries use for steering fragile Americana—George Washington's candlewick bedspread and John Quincy Adams's children's baptismal dresses, so fine they can almost be blown to bits by a sigh—through the perils of soap and water, there's only one simple principle to be faithfully observed. Frail materials must be provided with maximum

support at all times as they go through the washing process
to rout locked-in soil and restore freshness of color.

Prelaundry Testing

Before fabric is admitted to a "rocking" jar or a nylon-
mesh bag, the two guardians used against water weight, it
must pass a wash-worthy test. Faded food spots, hardened
fibers, places weakened by wear, should be wetted and exam-
ined, fingered, and judged. If any of these areas threatens to
disintegrate, the textile is deemed not sound enough to
undergo the rigors of washing, no matter how gentle that
may be.

Before you wash, also test the fabric for colorfastness.
Place it on a white blotter. Saturate a cotton swab with the
warm detergent solution you plan to use. Leave it on a color
area for five minutes or until the solution has thoroughly
penetrated, then blot with another white blotter. If there
is no color stain, wash as directed below. If there *is* a color
stain, try a solution made with cold water. If the color
doesn't run, wash as directed, using cold instead of warm
water. If the color does run, the only alternative is to send
the fabric to a dry-cleaner of the coddling type or to a
specialist in restoration.

Washing

Put bedspreads, tester valances, and other large pieces in
a nylon-mesh bag or a pillowcase, close with safety pins,
and swirl through suds made of one pint of pure Ivory
Flakes (the soap, not the detergent) dissolved in four gallons of warm water. The most convenient place to wash
large pieces is in the bathtub. For small pieces fill a one-
quart jar three-quarters full with three-quarters of an ounce
of soap flakes dissolved in warm water. Dissolve soap before
pouring it into the jar. Then gently rock the tightly capped

Washing heirloom fabric in a pillowcase

jar, supported by your hands at both ends, to and fro to agitate the water like a mini–washing machine.

Rinsing and Pampering

With little or no pressure, finger-drain out the soiled water and give the piece eight rinses—still in the jar or mesh bag. Experts at the Louise Hand Laundry in Washington, D.C., think it takes that many rinses to keep old materials from collecting scorch spots when ironed.

If the fabric still looks yellow after rinsing, they advise soaking it in a solution made of one cup of sodium perborate, a bleach available at drug stores, and one gallon of cold water. Remove it after fifteen minutes to examine it. If there are no unfavorable reactions, return textile to jar or mesh bag and repeat for another fifteen-minute period. Leave it in the solution no longer than half an hour. Follow with three rinsings: two warm and one cold. For the final, or bluing, rinse experiment with only a tiny bit of bluing strained into cold water and stirred to dissolve all particles. Watch the reaction of the textile to the bluing rinse. If you don't like the result, you can rinse out the bluing, and the fabric will still retain enough hint of bluing to make it look a little lighter and less yellow.

If the piece has long tassels or fringe that cannot be combed or brushed out, use a diaper softener mixed 1 part to 200 parts of tepid water (that is, two-thirds of an ounce of softener to one gallon of water). Let tassels or fringe soak for half an hour or until your fingers running through them encounter no snarls. Remove from the water, rinse, shake gently, and lay flat on a terry towel to dry.

Always remove a textile from a jar or mesh bag to a surface covered with large deep-pile towels. For even drying roll up textile firmly in several additional towels.

Ironing

Since your heirloom must be protected from its own weight during ironing, suspend one end of a large piece from a clothes hanger hung high above the ironing board; this takes weight off the other end. Better than an ironing board, of course, would be an enormous padded table—such as one hand laundry has for pressing an eleven-foot tablecloth—on which both large and small pieces can be

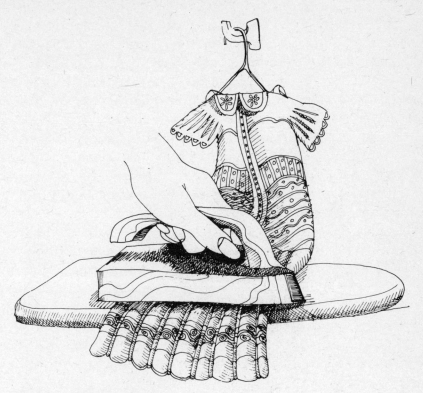

Ironing heirloom fabric

ideally spread out. Iron with the heat control at low and lay a piece of cotton or linen on the fabric to keep it from direct heat.

In many instances blocking can take the place of ironing. Spread the heirloom to dry on terry towels laid out on a flat surface. Use nonrust pins to shape and anchor the piece tautly but without strain.

SECOND METHOD

The plastic-screen method is used by museums to minimize handling of age-old pieces, such as an early nineteenth-century sampler or some other small treasure of cotton or linen embroidery or lace. Sandwich the sampler between two layers of plastic window screening (available in desired lengths at hardware stores). Buy enough so that you can cut it to extend a couple of inches beyond the edges of the sampler. When you are ready to wash the sampler, baste it all around with a running stitch to the two layers of plastic. This will hold it securely. Prepare a solution of one gallon of warm water and three ounces of a gentle detergent, one you customarily use for washing delicate fabrics. Before you wash, test the sampler for colorfastness, using the test described on page 126.

Fill a rust-free tray or washbasin with the detergent solution and lay the screen flat in it. Wash the sampler with a sponge, tamping, patting, and stroking lightly until it is clean on one side. Then turn it over and repeat the process. Go through a cycle of washing and rinsing, washing and rinsing, until the water is absolutely clear. Remove the screen from tray or basin and put it between two terry towels to absorb water.

When the sampler is almost dry, move it to the ironing board and take off the screening. Place the sampler wrong-side up on two thicknesses of terry toweling, and iron with a low-heat iron. Iron with a piece of cotton or linen placed over the sampler to keep the fabric from direct heat.

CHAPTER 21

Tinware (Tole)

OLD TIN TRAYS and other tinware—even with paint badly chipped and hand-painted roses and gold-leaf borders faded almost beyond recall—are relics of the eighteenth and nineteenth centuries which collectors are stumbling over one another to possess. These folk-art treasures of the past are also snapped up by young moderns who find the campy colors and bold designs as engaging as contemporary art.

Tinware, once itinerant peddlers' articles of barter, owes its renaissance to polished exhibits mounted by prestigious folk-art museums such as Sturbridge Village in Sturbridge, Massachusetts, and the Landis Valley Museum in Lancaster, Pennsylvania. Stylish artifacts at a recent show at New York's Museum of American Folk Art included a japanned coffeepot (imitating Japanese lacquer) with lively hand-painted roses, stenciled document boxes that once held valuable papers, painted tea caddies, children's alphabet plates, and trays.

RESTORING PAINTED TINWARE

If you've ever revived a fading design on a Hitchcock chair or a Pennsylvania Dutch dowry chest, then touching up a primitive decoration on old tinware should hold no terrors. To restore a decorated piece whose surface is crazed, chipped, and pitted and whose design is a ghost of its former glory, first, with a putty knife, scrape off only the background paint down to the metal, taking care to keep the painted design intact. Follow by rubbing with extra-fine steel wool. If the tin is rusty, wet the steel wool with kerosene. Wipe off residue with old rags. Discard the rags immediately after use, as an accumulation could result in spontaneous combustion. (For safe disposal of oily rags see suggestion in Chapter 11, "Iron," pages 85–86.)

If there are rusty surface pits to clean, dig into them with a probe—an orange stick or small dowel—wrapped in steel wool dipped in kerosene. Finally, wash the background with soap and water, rinse, and dry immediately to prevent rusting. Then repaint.

For repainting the background and touching up the decoration use artists'-quality antique oil colors for freehand painting. Available at art stores, these come already mixed to match or blend with the old tinware's original weathered colors. Let the restored piece stand for two or three weeks to dry thoroughly. Then coat it with clear varnish, which serves as a fixative for the restored decorations and helps to prevent rusting. The time element is important because drying of the varnish must begin at the top surface, not at the bottom, since there is no absorption by the metal. For more complicated techniques—of both freehand painting and stenciling—be guided by one of the excellent handbooks on traditional tinware painting.

CARE OF TINWARE

If your tin artifacts serve purely as decoration, clean them by washing with warm, soapy water, rinsing, and thoroughly drying. Don't use pressure when washing paint, or it may flake. A thin coating of clear wax will add surface luster, help keep the paint from cracking, and help preserve the metal.

If the tinware is in household use, handle it gently. Banging it about may flake off tin and chip the paint. Wash it as above, but do not use wax. When tinware is in daily use, the oil it picks up from the skin in handling does most of the things that wax does to preserve it.

Keep all tinware away from extremes of heat and cold. Don't set oven-heated serving plates, teakettles, or dishes of piping-hot food on tin trays. Don't scrub stubborn stains with harsh scouring powder; you may "wash out" oil paint and rub off gilt. Two methods will spruce up drab and shabby but sound pieces, revitalizing a lackluster design and enlivening fading color.

THE SOLVENT METHOD

Dampen a rag lightly with turpentine and wipe a small, inconspicuous area. If the test is successful, wipe the entire surface to clean off dirt. If the tinware reacts badly to the turpentine, however, use the second method.

THE STEEL-WOOL METHOD

Rub the finest of steel wools (000), which is hardly more abrasive than cotton, over the surface. It will dry-clean and refurbish any piece with safety. After using either method, wash, dry thoroughly, and apply a protective coating of clear wax, the final spruce-up touch.

CHAPTER 22

Wall Hangings

THE EMBROIDERED WALL HANGINGS handed down to us, from needlepoint to "needle paintings," rank high as decorations for today's interiors. Among these cherished pieces are early-American tapestries hand-woven in local factories under the supervisory eyes of the Royal Windsor Tapestry Works, of England, and of French master craftsmen brought here from Aubusson.

CARE OF HANGINGS

The secret of longevity for all wall hangings is weight-lifting. Fabulous Oriental scrolls and hangings have been able to defy the centuries because they were allowed to rest after periods of strain. Unrelieved strain on the warp of a piece will cause deterioration. When other furnishings are being put under dust covers for the summer is a good time to let wall hangings rest from their own weight.

Decorative textiles fragile with age need support on a wall. With cotton thread, tack across the back, at top and bottom, wide strips of muslin or webbing (such as upholsterers use). The strain will be eased even better by adding crisscross strips. Mount excessively fragile pieces on a complete backing of strong Dacron or Terylene net. Cut the coarse, strong net to the exact size of the hanging and tack it around the entire edge. Hang the textile by the net and stretch it tautly on the wall with tacks or nails. Be sure a hanging tapestry doesn't bunch in folds. When folds flatten out, they leave sharp creases that can cut threads.

MINOR REPAIRING

A timely stitch to close a slit, catch a runaway thread, or bind a raveling edge will save your hanging professional repairs. So will weft threads rewoven and a hole darned or patched.

HOME CLEANING

As soiled as wall hangings inevitably become, they need present no special challenge to home cleaning. Clean with a vacuum-cleaner brush if they cannot be washed—and many can be. The exceptions are tapestries too large to handle, those with bright clusters of yarn that are not dye-fast, and those that are brittle and have hardened spots.

As a test for possible color bleeding before you wash, try a few drops of any cleaning agent you propose to use on the several colors. Apply cleaner to one color, count to ten, cover with a folded white facial tissue, count to ten again, and observe tissue for any color staining. Repeat for every color. If none bleeds, go ahead with the washing. If any colors run, however, send the hanging to a reputable dry-cleaning specialist. He is also the expert to whom you can entrust an unwieldy but valuable hanging.

If the tapestry is colorfast and in good condition, wash with suds made from a gentle detergent of a type you ordinarily use for delicate fabrics. The solution should be 1 part detergent to 500 parts tepid water (1⅓ ounces of detergent to 5 gallons of water). Tamp, rather than rub, the hanging and turn it over and under as long as clean water applied to it becomes soiled. Move the piece in and out of several rinsings of warm distilled water. Press out all water, first with your hands, then with the tapestry wrapped in dry terry towels and lightly squeezed.

Before ironing, smooth out the tapestry to its proper shape, as you would do with a sweater you were blocking. Lay it right-side down and place a piece of cotton fabric on it to protect it from the iron's heat. Set the iron at low. If the tapestry is cushioned by thick terry towels, pressing will bring up the pattern.

CONTROLLING ROOM CLIMATE

Don't hang valuable tapestries or embroideries in strong sunlight or in a warm, damp, or poorly ventilated hall or foyer. To put up their best defense against mildew such heirlooms need a controlled climate, with a temperature between 60 and 65 degrees and a relative humidity around 50 per cent. Keep an eye out for furry patches, indicating mold growth. For what to do about it see "Mold" in Chapter 20, "Textiles," pages 124–125.

CHAPTER 23

Wooden Flooring

ALTHOUGH AN OLD HOUSE is not generally considered in the roster of antiques (such as statuary or fine paintings), it can be the most important treasure in its owner's collection. More than other beautiful and revered objects, however, an old house has its individual care problems. One of these is the upkeep of old floors, some of which may date back to Revolutionary times or before.

When early-American homes were built, the wide pine flooring boards were initially laid so tightly together that cracks between them were almost invisible. Cracks were so hairline fine, says the owner of a 1770 home, that even the ubiquitous sand spread on the floor instead of rugs in those days couldn't get into them. With the passing years, however, houses settle, and small crevices between floorboards enlarge so much that they become dirt-catching trenches.

WHAT TO DO ABOUT FLOORBOARD CRACKS

How can you dig centuries of soil out of these wide gaps, and how then can you keep them clean? One answer comes from the historic Jonathan Hasbrouck house in Newburgh, New York, a Dutch stone building dating back to 1750. It became General George Washington's headquarters, from which he commanded the Continental Army. Today it is a museum. The original fourteen-inch-wide pine boards still floor the main room and are a brilliantly waxed example of the marriage of modern technology and early-American construction.

First, the cracks in this floor were cleaned out with the floor attachment of a vacuum cleaner. If that doesn't work with your floor, try a stiff paintbrush with its bristles sliced thin enough to penetrate the crevices. If a third method is needed, scrape out the embedded dirt with a penknife.

Then the museum's maintenance staff filled the dirt-free cracks with Plastic Wood, a crack-filler available in natural pine and other wood colors. This can also be used to fill in gouges, holes, and scratches. When sanded down, it can make old floorboards as even as a carpenter's level. (See "Sources for Materials for the Care of Antiques," page 153.)

CARE AND UPKEEP

If the floor is waxed, dust with a fresh cotton (not an oil-treated) mop or the floor attachment of the vacuum cleaner. Polishing once every six weeks or so with a buffer or electric polisher will renew gleam, especially if a little fresh wax is applied beforehand to areas of the floor where the old wax is worn down.

If, however, you disdain modern finishes for your original wooden flooring and want to keep it as bare and clean as the day it was laid, use a broom to sweep it. Wash with a clean mop dipped in a pail of warm-water suds (made with a mild detergent) and wrung almost dry. Remove stains with a handbrush dipped into the suds. Rinse with clear, warm water, but be careful to rinse with the mop almost dry and to remove all soap.

CHAPTER 24

Woodenware (Treen)

MANY PEOPLE believe that the earliest American tableware was pewter, but woodenware, or treen (derived from "tree"), was in domestic use long before metal. In a pioneer home could be seen rows of polished tankards, goblets, bowls, ladles, pitchers, cups, and spoons hanging from a rack. The beakers from which our ancestors quaffed their toddies and the trenchers (plates or platters) from which two people could eat were among the ware carved from the hardwood of the region. Maple was the most popular wood, although birch, ash, oak, and black walnut were also commonly used. The wood had to be impenetrable and could not impart an unpleasant taste to food or drink. Lignum vitae—the hardest of all woods and valued for its impenetrability—boxwood, cedar, basswood, poplar, and other plentiful hardwoods often became deluxe tableware after being turned on a lathe and chiseled with ornamental designs.

This type of woodenware is gaining in popularity with collectors. In fact, they subdivide the field and specialize in certain categories of treen. One of the earliest collectors was Miles Standish, whose twelve trenchers, amassed in austere times, were considered an unseemly exhibit of worldly display.

SLIVER OF WOOD
WEDGED INTO CRACK

Finding a repair in a wooden bowl with a magnifying glass

CLEANING

Before cleaning these antique pieces, examine them under a strong magnifying glass to see if there are any fine lines indicating repairs. For example, you may find a section of carving replaced, a bowl restored to its pedestal, the insertion of a wooden sliver. If such repairs show up, even though they are almost invisible, don't wash the piece with soap and water, because the glue used for repair may be soluble. Clean with a natural-wax polish, used sparingly.

Where soap-and-water cleaning is permissible, use "dry" lather foam made from pure soap flakes and with a soft cloth briskly clean the wood. Rinse with another cloth moistened in clear water and wrung out almost dry. Dry thoroughly. Then rub with a soft polishing cloth or with your bare hands to bring up the wood's natural gleam. If cleaned well, wood will also show its decorative grain.

COMBATING INSECTS

If there are signs of insects—tiny holes bored into the wood—spray a household insecticide directly into the holes. Wipe off any surplus spray and set the piece aside to dry. Repeat the treatment as often as necessary. Never apply insecticides on utensils used for food: bowls, spoons, serving forks, ladles.

STORING

Stack treen in drawers or on cabinet shelves. Don't place objects on their sides, as this can cause warping. Don't store where dampness can make the wood swell and distort the shape of the pieces. Be sure the climate of the room where you store or display fragile old wood is neither too moist nor too dry. Protect it from the drying effects of steam heat even if you have to keep a container of water on the radiator.

CHAPTER 25

Keeping New Company

ANTIQUES MUST MEET the challenge of polished chrome and sparkling glass as they come cozily together with modern furnishings in today's rooms—another reason for the care they must get. The blending of the old and new which gives another dimension to antiques has gone beyond the glass-and-steel coffee table in front of a signed American Federal sofa. Molded chairs with clear glass sides and cartridge-type white leather upholstery add more smashing effects to the room. Bold abstract designs in upholstery fabrics are splashed all over early-American armchairs.

This new mix shows up on the walls, where Claes Oldenburg and Roy Lichtenstein share space with American primitive paintings or Currier and Ives prints. The contemporary room's steel-and-glass chill is killed by an eighteenth-century three-corner cupboard in one corner, a captain's table for playing backgammon in another. As long as the "mix" is kept in proper contrast—within its class instead of its period range—elegant old antiques blend superbly well with a Charles Eames lounge chair, and the mixture invigorates a traditional decor like a current of fresh air.

Bibliography

FOR MORE INFORMATION on the care and upkeep of antiques, the reader will find the following books helpful:

Davidson, Marshall B. *American Heritage History of Antiques from the Civil War to World War I*. New York: American Heritage Publishing Co., 1969.

Horton, Carolyn. *Cleaning and Preserving Bindings and Related Materials*. 2d ed. revised. Chicago: Library Technology Program, American Library Association, 1969.

Keck, Caroline K. *Care of Paintings: A Handbook*. New York: Watson-Guptill, 1965.

——. *How to Take Care of Your Pictures: A Primer of Practical Information*. New York: Museum of Modern Art and the Brooklyn Museum, 1965.

Mills, John Fitzmaurice. *The Care of Antiques*. London: Arlington Books, 1964.

Moore, Alma Chestnut. *How to Clean Everything*. New York: Simon and Schuster, 1968.

Plenderleith, H. J. *The Conservation of Antiquities and Works of Art*. London: Oxford University Press, 1962.

Reed, Jane M. *Art in the Home: How to Care for Your Valued Possessions.* St. Petersburg, Florida: The Stuart Society for the Museum of Fine Arts, 1968.

Savage, George. *The Art and Antique Restorers' Handbook.* Revised ed. New York: Praeger, 1967.

Seddon, Richard. *Art Collecting for Amateurs.* London: Frederick Muller Ltd., 1965.

Zigrosser, Carl, and Gaehde, Christa M. *A Guide to the Collecting and Care of Original Prints.* New York: Crown, 1969.

Sources for Materials for the Care of Antiques

OUTSIDE OF KNOWLEDGE and elbow grease, an indispensable ingredient in keeping antiques in good order is the use of various specialized products. There are so many efficient ones that it is impossible to include them all. If you cannot find a product that you are looking for, there's almost always another that will perform just as well. Listing those products of merit which are readily available and will be of great help to the reader does not indicate a guarantee or imply that others wouldn't do as good a job.

CHAPTER 1   ART IN THE HOME

Solander boxes (print storage cases). Available from The Mosette Co., 22 West 26th Street, New York, New York 10010.

Acid-free paper. Manufactured by Process Materials Corp., 329 Veterans Boulevard, Carlstadt, New Jersey 07075. Sold at art-supplies stores.

Acid-free cardboard. Manufactured by Bainbridge Sons, 20 Cumberland Street, Brooklyn, New York 11205. Sold at art-supplies stores.

Gummed linen or paper tape that adheres with cellulose paste. Manufactured and sold by Gummed Tape Corp., 147 West 15th Street, New York, New York 10011.

See-through sheets of clear acetate of .003 thickness. Manufactured by Celutone Plastics, Inc., 276 Park Avenue South, New York, New York 10010. Sold at art-supplies stores.

CHAPTER 2   LEATHER BOOKBINDINGS

Leather Protector (potassium-lactate solution). Mixed and sold by Technical Library Service, 104 Fifth Avenue, New York, New York 10011.

Krylon No. 1301. Manufactured by Borden Chemical Co., Consumer Products Division, 350 Madison Avenue, New York, New York 10017. Sold at art-supplies stores.

Pink Pearl Erasers No. 101. Manufactured by Eberhard Faber, Inc., Crestwood, Wilkes-Barre, Pennsylvania 18703. Sold at art-supplies and stationery stores.

CHAPTER 4   CRYSTAL CHANDELIERS

Omit. Sold by Peerless Camera Shop, 415 Lexington Avenue, New York, New York 10016.

Weiman's Chandelier Cleaner. Manufactured by Herbert Stanley, Westmoreland Building, Old Orchard Road, Skokie, Illinois 60079. Sold in housewares sections of department stores.

Small wire pins (hooks) and wire by the yard. Sold by the Gem, Monogram & Cut Glass Corp., 623 Broadway, New York, New York 10012.

Chapter 7 Furniture

Renuzit Spot Remover. Manufactured by Renuzit Home Products Co., 3018 Market Street, Philadelphia, Pennsylvania 19104. Sold at hardware stores and in housewares sections of department stores.

Krylon No. 1301. Manufactured by Borden Chemical Co., Consumer Products Division, 350 Madison Avenue, New York, New York 10017. Sold at art-supplies stores.

Synvar. Manufactured by the Weber Co., Wayne and Windrum Avenues, Philadelphia, Pennsylvania 19144. Sold at paint-supply and hardware stores.

10 per cent potassium-lactate solution. Mixed and sold by Technical Library Serivce, 104 Fifth Avenue, New York, New York 10011.

Reproductions of early-American upholstery fabrics: seven patterns authorized for reproduction by the American Wing of the Metropolitan Museum of Art. Available at Brunschwig & Fils, Inc., 979 Third Avenue, New York, New York 10022.

Reproductions of eighteenth-century historic Newport and eighteenth-century documentary Williamsburg fabrics. Available at F. Schumacher & Co., 919 Third Avenue, New York, New York 10022.

Chapter 11 Iron

Rustoleum paint in regular and aerosol cans and Rustoleum primer in regular and aerosol cans. Manufactured by the Rustoleum Corp., 2301 Oakton, Evanston, Illinois 60204. Sold at hardware and paint-supply stores.

CHAPTER 13   MARBLE AND SLATE

Goddard Marble Polish. Manufactured by J. Goddard & Sons, a subsidiary of Johnson Wax Co., Racine, Wisconsin 53400. Sold in housewares sections of department stores.

Marble Care Kits. Manufactured and sold by Vermont Marble Co., Proctor, Vermont 05765. Write directly to this supplier for product and price list.

Lemon Oil Polish. Manufactured by Chemicals by Bilco Co., 607 DeGraw Street, Brooklyn, New York 11217. Sold at hardware stores and in housewares sections of department stores.

CHAPTER 15   PAPIER-MÂCHÉ

Goddard Furniture Cream. Manufactured by J. Goddard & Sons, a subsidiary of Johnson Wax Co., Racine, Wisconsin 53400. Sold in housewares sections of department stores.

Impregnated silver-polish cloth. Manufactured by W. & J. Hagerty & Sons, 1204 Woodward Avenue, South Bend, Indiana 46613. Sold in housewares sections of department stores.

Elmer's Glue All. Manufactured by Borden Chemical Co., 350 Madison Avenue, New York, New York 10017. Sold at stationers and art-material and school-supply stores.

CHAPTER 18   RUGS

Liquid Latex (Saf-T-Bak) and Non-Skid Rug Backing. Distributed by Testworth Laboratory, Inc., Addison, Illinois 60101. Available from Sears, Roebuck catalog (see listing in carpet section).

CHAPTER 19   SILVER

Silver Care. Manufactured by J. Goddard & Sons, a subsidiary of Johnson Wax Co., Racine, Wisconsin 53400. Sold at hardware stores and in housewares sections of department stores.

Silver Foam. Manufactured by W. & J. Hagerty & Sons, 1204 Woodward Avenue, South Bend, Indiana 46613. Sold at hardware stores and in housewares sections of department stores.

CHAPTER 20   TEXTILES

Sodium perborate (a bleach). Manufactured by Purepac Corporation, 200 Elmora Avenue, Elizabeth, New Jersey 07200. Available at drug stores.

CHAPTER 23   WOODEN FLOORING

Plastic Wood. Manufactured by Boyle-Midway, Inc., a division of American Home Products Corp., South Avenue and Hale, Cranford, New Jersey 07016. Sold at hardware and paint-supply stores and supermarkets.

Index